SM00004946
5 |01
£15-°

Reflections on pra

Series editor: Richard Johnstone

The views expressed in this book are those of the editor and contributors and do not necessarily reflect the views of CILT.

REFLECTIONS ON PRACTICE

Editorial Committee
Professor Richard Johnstone, University of Stirling
Professor Chris Brumfit, University of Southampton
Professor Michael Byram, University of Durham
Ute Hitchin, CILT
Dr Lid King, CILT
Paul Meara, University College of Swansea
Dr Rosamond Mitchell, University of Southampton
Antony Peck, University of York
David Westgate, University of Newcastle-upon-Tyne

First published 1995
Copyright © 1995 Centre for Information on Language Teaching and Research
ISBN 1 874016 48 8

Cover by Neil Alexander
Printed in Great Britain by Bourne Press Ltd

Published by the Centre for Information on Language Teaching and Research, 20 Bedfordbury, Covent Garden, London WC2N 4LB.

Contents

Preface

Reflections on reading is the second title in CILT's REFLECTIONS ON PRACTICE series. The series was launched by *Language teaching in the mirror*, edited by Antony Peck and David Westgate, which develops and exemplifies the concept of the reflective practitioner as applied to the domain of modern language teaching.

As David Westgate puts it, a reflective approach:

> '*offers a perspective in which teachers come to take it as read that aspects of what they do merit their professional curiosity and that they have the capacity, as professionals, to gather and take account of some relevant evidence.*'
>
> *(Language teaching in the mirror: 1)*

Reflection can often be prompted by a desire for self-improvement. In this sense, when working with student-teachers who were in the process of developing habits of reflection, Antony Peck found it useful to address with them questions such as:

> '*Do you think carefully about your teaching? Which aspects of your language teaching do you reflect on most? How do you organise your self-evaluation? Have you noticed any improvements?*'
>
> *(Language teaching in the mirror: 63)*

In the same title, Diana Kent draws attention to the concurrent nature of 'doing' and 'reflecting' — that is, the reflection is undertaken by busy practitioners who inevitably often work under severe pressure of time. For her, a reflective approach is not about the development and testing out of some abstract theoretical proposition about language teaching, but rather:

> '. . . what is essential is the consciousness of one's practical theory and that it should be a theory constantly subjected to testing and refinement throughout one's working life.'
> *(Language teaching in the mirror: 61)*

Among the procedures for gathering data about one's 'practical theory' of teaching that are explained and exemplified in David Westgate and Antony Peck's first title are:

- diary keeping;
- mutual observation;
- discussion;
- use of observation schedules;
- analysis of audio- or video-recordings;
- descriptive logs;
- reciprocal (peer) observation, whether by teachers or students.

Mike Calvert argues that data-gathering procedures such as the above can fit into a wider action-research cycle, involving a series of steps that practitioners can take:

> '. . . looking at an area of teaching and developing an area they want to, need to and feel able to change; defining a clear goal which can be achieved within a relatively short period of time; setting out a plan of work and a realistic timetable; finding out ways of recording what is happening; analysing the findings and evaluating successes and failures; hypothesising on reasons for success and extending the ideas as they think fit to other classes and situations.'
> *(Language teaching in the mirror: 80)*

Reflections on reading, the present second title in the series, exemplifies very well the principles and practice of reflective teaching as set out above. The three main contributors are teachers who were interested in how to help their students bridge the enormous gap between GCSE and 'A' level, particularly in respect of the reading of literary texts. It may be worthy of note that all three acknowledge the benefits of postgraduate study at Masters level in encouraging them to develop their own particular ways of reflecting on their practice.

Jane Roots, Patricia Rees and Liliane White have therefore not only written up their work for university academic purposes but have also adapted it for present purposes. I am very grateful to them for their double effort and achievement in doing so, and also to Mike Grenfell who as editor of the present title was an indispensable link between the writers and the publisher.

Professor Richard Johnstone
Series editor: REFLECTIONS ON PRACTICE

Introduction

by Michael Grenfell

The changing place of reading

Reading has occupied an ambivalent position in the teaching of modern languages. Under traditional systems such as 'O' level, grammar-translation methods focused on developing foreign languages as an extension of general literacy gained in primary and secondary education. Work concentrated on memorising vocabulary, learning grammatical rules and translating sense and style from one language to the other. Reading was central to this approach, as it was by reading that pupils analysed language and committed it to memory. It was through reading that teachers tested comprehension as a means of assessing linguistic competence. Implicit in this approach was a model of learning that saw language as a series of building blocks. Pupils constructed their foreign language by putting together small units and making ever larger sequences. Oral skills were seen as subsidiary to this process; even listening tests were based on the reading out of short narratives similar to those used in translation exercises. The natural extension of such an approach in sixth form examinations such as 'A' level required concentrated analysis on literary texts, and harder and harder translation exercises.

Communicative language teaching (CLT) changed all that. It is difficult to exaggerate the impact of CLT on modern language teaching and syllabus design. Translation was out. Grammar analyses were complementary rather than central to developing linguistic competence. Oral/aural skills were now the focus for classroom practice. Firstly through the graded objectives movement and then in GCSE, transactional language was the order of the day: pupils learnt how to get things done in real contexts, how to negotiate social situations and find out what they needed to know. In this way, the social interactional approach of CLT eclipsed the literary skills of 'O' level and similar systems.

Unsurprisingly, in the rush to create communicative classrooms with a high use of target language and with role plays, information gaps and listening tasks, reading has been pushed out. There appear to have been three reasons for this:

- it was seen as **complementary,** as a source of information in such authentic materials as restaurant menus, posters, train times, road signs and the like;
- it was regarded as **passive,** as something that did not need to be taught but was acquired as part of general oral/aural competence;
- it became **peripheral,** an activity used to test comprehension or as a filler for the times when the teacher was away from class.

Published textbooks have mostly followed this trend with their concentration on short reading passages for information retrieval. With a few exceptions, extended reading material has been rare.

Reading in the first language: phonics and real books

If reading has been overlooked in second language teaching, the situation has been quite the reverse in the case of the first language. Here, reading, and hence the way it is taught, goes to the very heart of the education debate on what happens in our schools. Reading ability is often taken as a measure of a pupil's maturity and intellectual development. Underachievement in reading in the early years is seen as a hindrance to pupils for the rest of their school lives. It is unsurprising, therefore, that how reading is taught in English lessons should be so hotly contested. In the 1990s there has been the emergence of two opposing camps:

- those who believe that **phonics** is the best means to learning how to read; and
- the advocates of **real books**.

Phonics accords very much with the 'common sense' view of learning to read, which is understood to be the sequential **decoding** of letters, words, sentences and paragraphs. Sense is derived from such decoding.

Real books on the other hand are based on an **apprenticeship** model of learning, as pupils acquire competence through the **relationship** they build up with books. With real books children are expected to bring their own world views, emotions, experiences, etc to the task of reading and to develop skills through the use of contexts and clues found in the text.

This practical debate is underpinned by theory and research in the academic world. Back in 1967 Goodman undermined the common sense view of reading by arguing that it should be regarded essentially as a 'psycholinguistic guessing game', which involves an active, purposeful reader. Other research has shown how the mature reader's eyes do not move in a linear 'decoding' direction but are constantly darting back and forth, up and down, as the brain searches for and constructs meaning for itself. In another classic study, Smith (1982) argued that reading is a construction of questions and hypotheses about the text that are answered by the relationship that forms between what readers see and the knowledge of the world they already have in their brains.

This approach to reading is very naturalistic as it somewhat opposes the instructional view of phonics which can be understood as the application of explicit learning. If the latter is seen as a **bottom-up** decoding of letters, the naturalistic approach is very much **top-down,** as it involves the whole learner and the context of reading besides the letters on the page.

Reading in a foreign language

It is easy to draw parallels between the debate in the last section and changes in modern language learning and teaching. On the one hand, there are resonances between the naturalistic character of CLT and the holistic approach to reading. On the other hand, there are direct links between the explicit knowledge required of phonics in learning to read and the role of grammar in learning a foreign language. Indeed, so strong is the intuitive naturalness of CLT and real books that it is easy to overstate the methodological conclusions to be drawn from them. The natural end of communicative and reading competence has come to be viewed as also the means to that end. Yet, a degree of caution is necessary. In the case of reading, Perera (1978) was one of the first to point out how misleading it can be to over-generalise from the skilled to the beginner reader. In a similar way, we might comment that the current push for maximal target language use in the classroom assumes that learners can induce rules in much the same way that they did in learning their first language. Such a view overlooks the language skills learners already possess through their first language, how these may be drawn upon, and the capacity to think and reflect about language that is not available when they are acquiring this first language in the first place.

Many aspects from the reading debate in English do, however, transfer to the context of foreign language learning and teaching. These may be summed up in the following issues:

- the degree to which learners read by decoding in a linear manner, and the degree to which they involve their whole world knowledge and experiences;
- the extent to which contexts and clues are used in making sense of texts;
- how pupils match sounds to letters, store them, and systematise on the basis of these;
- the reasons learners read: for information, evaluation, pleasure, etc;

- the personal choices made by readers in selecting texts and how to read them;
- how to teach these skills.

What is clear is that most readers have developed some degree of literacy skill when they come to reading in the foreign language. This is a help. For the most part, European letter combinations are the same, cultural conventions are similar and reading is, to a greater or lesser extent, already an aspect of life. Yet, literacy skills can also be a hindrance. Although letter combinations look the same, they do not make sense in the same way. Cognates are of use, but they can also mislead. What is heard and what is seen do not equate in the way that they do in English. As a consequence, many of the previously acquired literacy skills are disrupted. The text can become a 'noise' within which it is difficult to make sense.

The role of reading in learning a foreign language

The thrust of communicative language teaching as described above has often avoided confronting these problems. It has done this implicitly by focusing on the oral/aural in teaching and using reading mainly for information retrieval. A key aspect of such reading has been to scan and skim for required detail, overlooking the mass of what is not understood. Such is the logic of pupil as host or tourist; where reading is limited to the pragmatic task in hand.

Yet such an approach, besides leaving undeveloped skills that are integral to a mature linguistic competence, overlooks the role that reading may have in language learning as a whole:

- Even as extreme an advocate of the 'natural approach' as Krashen (1984) sees reading as an excellent source of **comprehensible input.**
- Moreover, the written word reinforces and supports what pupils say and hear. It helps therefore to construct that internal system that is necessary to a fully generative competence in a language.
- Finally, if we are to see language as a personal skill, as a means of expressing identity in an independent way, then reading offers a means, par excellence, of enhancing autonomy and a sense of self in relation to that new language.

This book contains three extensive reflections by practising teachers who have addressed the issue of reading. Each arises from a concern to do something about the way that reading is being under-used in contemporary modern language learning.

The first reflection by **Jane Roots** involves her enquiry into the reading habits of her Year 9 German sets. She begins by comparing her pupils' reading in English and German. In the course of questioning her pupils Jane reflects on how she currently approaches reading with her beginner groups, and notes the limited nature of the reading tasks with which she presents them. She then explains how, on the basis of this case study, she intends to set about enhancing reading for a wider range of purposes.

This reflection focuses on learners as they move from beginner to intermediate levels in secondary school foreign language learning. It highlights, perhaps unsurprisingly, that reading tasks at this level have so far been mainly concerned with literal meaning and sound/print correspondences.

The next two reflections both address the move from intermediate to advanced levels.

Pat Rees explores the previous reading habits of her students in the first year of sixth form, and identifies the difficulties they have in encountering literary texts for the first time. In some respect, it is at this level that 'serious' language work begins and Pat's data show students struggling both to find their own voice in the language and to develop the sort of skills necessary to help them with advanced texts. The gap from GCSE to sixth form is seen to be enormous, and both teachers and students work to compensate in the areas in which they experience difficulties.

Many of the points raised by Pat are expanded upon and given illustration in **Liliane White's** case studies. Liliane has interviewed both teachers and students in three sixth form colleges in order to uncover attitudes to reading. However, she also spent time in lessons to find out what was going on in practice. What she catalogues gives us insight into what works and why — and what does not work and why — in using printed texts in the classroom.

The three contributions shed much light on the state of reading under current syllabus and methodological design. Each teacher acts as a reflective practitioner. Each uses a range of methods and approaches to construct their reflection. Each draws out the methodological implications of what they have seen and heard. In the final chapter to this book, I make these implications explicit in a formal way. I refer to the way the three contributors have gone about their reflections, and suggest ways in which others might follow them in their concern to develop reading in modern language teaching and learning in UK schools.

References

Goodman K S, 'Reading: a psycholinguistic guessing game' (1967) in Gollasch F V (ed), *Language and literacy: the selected writings of Kenneth S Goodman*, vol 1 (Routledge and Kegan Paul, 1982)

Krashen S, *Writing: research, theory and applications* (Pergammon, 1984)

Perera K, Review of Smith F, 'Reading' (1978) in *Journal of linguistics*, no. 16: 127–31 (Cambridge University Press, 1980)

Smith F, *Understanding reading,* 3rd edition (New York: Holt, Rinehart and Winston, 1982)

Chapter 1

Reading: from beginners to intermediate

by Jane Roots

In my classroom as, I expect, in many language classrooms, there is a small bookcase containing some readers in French and the occasional one in German in pristine condition. One or two of the books with animal pictures on the front cover are slightly shabby and the *Lesekiste* box — published by Mary Glasgow Publications — showing signs of wear: probably from the times I or a colleague have been absent from school and the books have been given to the pupils; or where there have been a few minutes spare in the lesson and reading has been used to fill this; or perhaps given to pupils as holiday reading. Reading somehow slotted into these sorts of occasions in many language classrooms.

Three years ago the staple diet in my classroom, as I suspect in many others, tended to be the textbook. In terms of reading this offered short items requiring mainly comprehension practice based on question and answers. These exercises were mainly presented as a series of problem solving activities. There seemed to be few opportunities for pupil involvement with texts, extensive reading or reading as a means to other more creative work.

The case study I carried out was a preliminary stage in trying to move away from reading purely for comprehension. I felt that if I could find out more about what pupils' reading habits, likes and dislikes were, it would enable me to work on fostering a wider range of reading activities in my classroom.

There seemed many more reasons **against** than **for** such a move, including:

- lack of time;
- lack of suitable material;
- lack of motivation amongst staff and pupils towards reading.

But I was determined to make reading a much more significant part of my classroom practice, and to show that literature can have a place in foreign language teaching in an eleven to sixteen comprehensive school.

A NARROW EXPERIENCE OF READING

It was clear to me that GCSE-type language materials had shaped a good deal of what went on in modern language lessons throughout the school. Despite the equal weighting of the four skills, reading seemed to play a minor role in classrooms. It is a skill that deals with the comprehension of authentic text and little else; whether a student can decipher a train timetable, read a menu, or understand a shopping list. This narrow experience of reading and the total absence of literature is perhaps understandable in the focused environment of preparing for public examinations. Yet, it was apparent that such treatment of reading created a number of problems, not least of which was the jump students had to make when embarking on 'A' level studies. Moreover, there seemed no reason why reading, particularly extensive reading, might not be used throughout the school.

This case study deals with two classes of Year 9 pupils learning German. They amounted to 48 pupils in all, who had been studying German for almost three years. They were, therefore, just about to commence their GCSE course.

A PIECE OF ACTION RESEARCH

The formal framework for my work with these pupils was provided by my studies for a MA in Language and Education at Southampton University. Having studied the various aspects of language learning and teaching, I was keen to develop the ideas this had given to me in my own practical context. The full study was written up and presented as my dissertation for awarding this degree. The work can be considered as a piece of action research. Before embarking on administering questionnaires to my pupils, I again looked at the coursebooks I had been using with them. I also referred to the academic research on reading. I wanted to know more about what pupils looked for in textbooks and what students read for pleasure.

PROBLEMS WITH TEXTBOOKS

While reconsidering textbooks as a source of reading materials, I was reminded of what one pupil had recently said to me:

> *'The passages given in textbooks are only what people who write them think you ought to learn, introducing one piece of vocabulary at a time. The 'books' (referring to story books) make you think and look at vocabulary more.'*

I thought that this echoed rather well the situation Krashen had described:

> 'The only reading many foreign language students encounter are paragraphs that are loaded up with complex vocabulary and syntax. It is nearly always grammatically sequenced: writers are careful to include syntax that the student is supposed to have studied or is correctly learning.' (Krashen, 1982)

Both of these statements seemed a fair description of the kind of textbooks I had been using.

- Most problematic, it seemed to me, was the way coursebooks contained exercises which tended to **concentrate on the sentence**, or even smaller units than the sentence. Pupils were encouraged to understand every word. In this situation, as soon as there was too much information, 'noise' as Frank Smith calls it, the learner easily becomes dissuaded from reading. He or she will be frightened to skip words and will have to understand each one. Even in more modern books, which made extensive use of authentic texts, there were often few pictures or other accompanying clues to aid pupil comprehension, and little that could be considered 'reading for pleasure'.

- My pupils had **little choice** over even the coursebooks they were given. It was I who prepared the schemes of work and chose the coursebooks that would supplement or lead my teaching. In this I made choices concerning which books and materials would suit my purposes.

I was struck at the time by a piece of research from the University of Keele. Workers there had asked a group of mixed ability children in three year groups (7, 9 and 10) to rate whether they found each of the fourteen features of textbooks to be helpful, to make no difference, or to be unhelpful in their reading. These results (see p10) confirmed my belief, partly endorsed by my pupils in discussion with them, that layout and format were extremely important in making texts reader-friendly. It also highlighted for me a number of other issues concerning what to look out for in choosing books.

THE CONTRIBUTION OF READING FOR PLEASURE

My real concern, however, was to consider what reading for pleasure might contribute to foreign language lessons. I had an image in my mind that I found articulated again by Krashen:

> 'The sort of reading to be analysed here is extensive and concerns subject matter that the student would read in his first language for pleasure. It is completely voluntary . . . readers have the option of skipping whole sections they find either too difficult or less interesting. They even have the option of putting the book down and selecting another after reading only a few

pages. *They can skip words they do not understand, if they think they are following the main points and they have the option, of course, of looking up every word, if that is their style . . . the only requirement is that the story or main idea be comprehensive and that the topic be something the student is genuinely interested in, that he would read in his own language.'* (Krashen, 1982: 164)

The above picture now seems a little idealistic. But I wondered if there were ways of transferring these types of language skill and habit from first to their second language learning. My action research took place in two main phases: first a questionnaire study, then the development of a reading progression programme.

Features of textbooks found helpful by mixed ability classes

Rank	Feature	Helpful	No difference	Unhelpful
01	Headings	71	28	01
02	Section to tell you what the chapter is about	69	29	02
03	Short chapters	68	29	03
04	Cartoons	68	25	02
05=	Use of colour to show important points	63	34	02
05=	Use of underlining to show important points	63	34	02
07	Photographs	63	30	07
08	Spacious layout	54	39	07
09	Sub-headings	53	41	06
10	Tables	48	40	11
11	Section to remind you what the chapter was about	47	45	06
12	Graphs	44	43	13
13	Questions at end of each chapter	41	46	13
14	Suggestions for further reading	40	47	13

% endorsing (n = 87)

From: Teacher's weekly 09.11.89

Phase One: Questionnaire Study

What I wanted to find out

What then was of interest to my pupils in 1990, in their third year of studying German? To sum up: I wanted to establish —

- what the students read in their own language;
- how much time they spent on reading;
- what might induce them to extend the time that they spend on reading;
- to compare this with their habits in German as a way of finding links for a way forward in improving reading habits as part of their language learning.

The following questionnaire was given to all pupils in two parallel German classes without reference to each other:

Questionnaire for pupils

READING QUESTIONNAIRE
Please answer the following questions:

ENGLISH

1. How often do you read outside the formal classroom setting?
   Per day/per week? Time in minutes.
2. What do you read?
3. How often do you read for pleasure?
   Per day/per week? Time in minutes.
4. What do you read?
   I would increase the amount of my reading if . . .

GERMAN

5. How often do you read German outside the classroom?
   Per day/per week? Time in minutes.
6. What do you read?
7. How often do you read German for pleasure?
   Per day/per week? Time in minutes.
8. What do you read?
   I would increase my amount of reading in German if . . .

THANK YOU!

Results

The results are as follows:

Reading in English outside the formal classroom setting (Q1)

Number of students	Minutes per day	Number of students	Minutes per day
01	10	08	60
03	20	02	90
05	40	03	120
07	50		

Of the 42 students who replied, only one admitted to reading less than 15 minutes per day. Some qualified their answers instead of giving a specific time:

03	fairly often
02	twice a week, up to an hour
02	three hours a week
01	monthly(ish); every day; two hours a week; usually every night; every evening.

As the students were not asked to give their name, I felt the skew effect of wanting to enhance their answer to please or cause displeasure was minimalised, although as the students were not in complete isolation there could be some peer pressure.

What students read in English (Q2)

Number of students	What they read	Number of students	What they read
02	set books	05	anything
03	adventures	06	newspapers
03	thrillers	13	books
03	short stories	14	novels
04	comics	25	magazines

There were several cases in which one single student mentioned a particular item: books about prejudice and justice in the world; articles; poems; political sagas; historical sagas; espionage; biographies; computer manuals; fact books; science fiction; letters.

How often students read for pleasure (Q3)

Number of students	Minutes per day approximately	Number of students	Minutes per day approximately
03	10	04	50
03	20	03	60
10	30	04	120
01	40		

Others qualified their answers:

03	every day
02	all the time
01	2 hours per week; every evening; 2/4 days per week; often; sometimes per day; it is always for pleasure, I am not forced to read; 3 hours a week.

What students read for pleasure (Q4)

Number of students	What they read for pleasure
03	books
04	newspapers
04	novels
11	magazines

In several cases, one student mentioned a particular item: adventure; comedy; fantasy; football; science fiction; supernatural; books; cereal packets; toothpaste tubes.

Seventeen students said 'see Question 2', wrote 'anything' in both Q2 and Q4 or wrote the same items in Q2 and Q4. These students largely did not distinguish between reading for pleasure and reading.

Four students distinguished between Q2 and Q4 by qualifying the noun:

Q2 magazines	Q4 computer magazines
Q2 books	Q4 football books
Q2 coursebooks	Q4 supernatural books
Q2 magazines	Q4 football/cricket magazines

**Students would increase their amount of reading
in English if . . . (Q4)**

Number of students	If ...
03	there was more reading homework/was set reading to do
03	they had to
05	they didn't have so much homework
28	they had more/enough time

There were several cases in which one student mentioned a specific condition: had no TV; wider range of books available; more exciting books available; spent more time at home; had more books; knew it would help my education; saw it had a severe effect on my written work, which it doesn't at the moment.

The above findings would reflect the growing concern amongst teachers of Year 10 students that time is a major problem for them, either as a result of too much coursework and homework, or as a result of the influence of 'experiencing the world' and a failure to commit themselves to work.

Reading in German

I then turned to a section about reading in German and asked the same questions. The responses make depressing reading but perhaps a basis to work on.

How often students read in German outside the classroom (Q5)

Number of students	How often they read in German outside the classroom
02	when they had to
02	1 hour per week
02	30 minutes per week
03	when given magazines in German
03	15 minutes or more
03	3 hours per week
06	never
06	every day
10	hardly ever

There were several cases in which one student responded: depends on amount of work; 2 hours a week; don't read much; varies; 10 minutes; 3 times a month; but I watch Satellite TV in German; not regularly; only as work; only penfriend letters.

It was disappointing that sixteen students read either hardly ever or not at all, but I believe these comments may have resulted from the following causes:

*   wishing to cause pleasure or displeasure to me!
*   making some comment about homework.

The students regularly complain about having too much homework in German (and I suspect in other subjects too). It shows perhaps a need for a more structured approach to homework and reading. It also shows that indeed not a great demand is placed on them in reading.

What students read in German (Q6)

Number of students	What they read	
02	penfriend letters	
04	homework	There were three cases in which one student mentioned a specific item: dictionaries; books; German reading books.
16	magazines	
27	textbooks	

The students are all issued with a textbook, used particularly for reference. It is the one source of material that they have with them during the whole course. Dictionaries, magazines and some books are available in the classroom.

How often students read in German for pleasure (Q7)

Number of students	How often	
02	twice a week, up to an hour	There were four cases in which one student responded: every night; 5 minutes per day; once a month; when I've time.
03	30 minutes per week	
05	only occasionally	
05	hardly ever	
17	never	

This was most depressing, but coupled with the results from Q8 led me to feel that the task of finding material for them would be worthwhile as I felt there was indeed fertile ground here.

What students read in German for pleasure (Q8)

Number of students	What they read for pleasure	
02	letters from penfriends	There were several cases in which one student responded: nothing; *Winnie the Pooh* and *Garfield;* the only books in German I own; I haven't anything to read for pleasure; a book given when in Germany; texts in exercise book.
03	magazines	
05	*Juma*	
05	textbooks	

Twenty-eight students failed to give an answer here or wrote N/A, or *see above.* At this stage the only materials easily available to them were the *Juma* magazine, a few German magazines sent from our partner school and a series of readers. Few of them made use of the materials available.

Students would increase their amount of reading in German if . . . (Q8)

Number of students	If ...
02	it was interesting
02	I could read and enjoy it more
03	they were more accessible to me
03	we had to do it for homework
04	I had more time
04	there were more magazines
05	I could understand it better
13	I had access to books

There were 13 aspects which were mentioned once. These included: having to increase reading; I enjoyed it more.

Conclusion

The questionnaires were completed by almost all of my pupils. The results showed that:

- in their mother tongue they were generally regular readers, although certain constraints such as time meant that some of them were not regular readers for pleasure;
- in German they were not regular readers, with more than 72% (26) failing to read regularly, and just 13 admitting to reading for pleasure.

Taking the number of students who specified a time for reading for pleasure (Q3) in the mother tongue, the average was 46 minutes per day per student. Reading in Q1 resulted in 59 minutes per day. It appeared therefore that for this particular group of students, 78% of their total reading time was reading for pleasure in their mother tongue.

These results clearly did not give numerical proof for specific conclusions. However, they showed me that there was much to suggest that the task of matching students and materials, although not at all an easy one to contemplate, would be worthwhile. The students' responses, particularly in Q2 and Q4 gave me ideas about the sorts of materials that I needed to find for them.

PHASE TWO: DEVELOPING A READING PROGRESSION PROGRAMME

On the basis of these findings, I decided to develop a **Reading Progression Programme** for pupils in the first years of language learning. For me this entailed:

- first, finding ways of encouraging the **matching of sound and symbol or pictures** in early language learning;
- second, developing exercises to **increase confidence** in dealing with texts at a later stage.

Both of these seemed important in developing the use of reading texts in the early secondary school years, as well as GCSE courses.

Matching of sound and symbol or pictures

CARDS, PICTURES AND TAPES

Obviously, the process of identification of different combinations of letters with sound is at the centre of matching written forms of the language with what has been heard. I had noticed that there were a number of letter groupings which cause children problems in their own tongue, and that there are different ones in the various foreign languages. The alphabetical sound which is produced very early in my classroom, and one which is frequently referred to, can be at variance with the usage of that letter. In the German language, for example, the letter *v* has its alphabetical sound *fau,* but may have the sound *var,* as in the English *vase,* attached to it. I felt that I wanted to reach the stage where the sound/graphic combination was established, not just for the purposes of 'reading aloud', but for the child to be able to reach the point where the spoken word is his or her guide to the printed word.

To encourage this I introduced a system of cards with pictures on them and accompanying tapes produced by our German assistant. These were based on the classroom instructions that we used in class, so that the pupils could match sounds and symbols. For example, I used a picture of a door being closed and the phrase *Mach die Tür zu* on tape. I used magazine pictures, sketches from myself and pupils; indeed, any materials available which gave a clear message. Each of the texts was recorded on a short-length tape in order to make them easily accessible to the pupils. I used the peripheral laboratory system in my classroom to enable the students to be in control of their learning.

PUPPETS

Another strategy that I used to encourage early cognitive development was work with puppets, where again the links between action and sound could be exploited. As a group, the pupils developed puppets ranging from simple pictures stuck on straws to sock puppets with a variety of scenes as backcloths; initially to extend the previous activity with classroom scenes as a backdrop. They could then use a copy of the tape produced previously, or their own voices to re-enact instructions. I found that this was an extremely good technique, in particular with younger children, as they were less inhibited in using their voices.

STORY PLUS PICTURE

Part of my teaching has always been the use of story and picture. Stories such as the *Easter Bunny* have been used at the appropriate time of year. I always link these with my own sketches, which, I have to admit, are generally crude. Yet, this very crudeness has at least one advantage over the slick, commercial equivalents. As one of my pupils was heard to remark: '*With her pictures, it's once seen never forgotten.*' I try to make the stories live, through actions, sketches and my choice of words. Phrases from the story are then put on to the overhead projector, and students are asked to match them to the appropriate part of the action. The story is not told particularly slowly, but, inevitably, with the actions and sketches, the overall time taken to deliver the story can be quite lengthy. One of the advantages I find of doing this is that because I do not read the story, the phrases I use are different from the printed pupils' version.

ASCERTAINING THE LEVEL OF DEPENDENCE ON ILLUSTRATIONS

In another example of the use of story and text in my classroom, I tried to ascertain the level of dependence on the illustration and other accompanying clues. I chose *Alfi, der Superpiep* and read it to a group of pupils. This is a book with a simple storyline, bright pictures and a number of explosive situations, which lent itself well to this exercise. After reading the story to the Year 9 pupils, I asked them about the story, what they had heard, noticed and seen, and what they had understood.

Their replies fell into four categories that showed me how the pupils had 'read' the story:

* total reliance on the words of the story;
* reliance on the picture coupled with recognition of isolated words and actions;
* some understanding of the words of the storyline with reinforcement from the visual and sound patterns;
* words of the story working together with the picture to form a whole, explosive words merely reinforcing understanding.

I was struck by how important it was to remember that, given the individual language abilities of pupils, all of these were likely to be occurring at one time in my class as I read it out loud to them. Several of the pupils asked if they could read the story themselves. Some commented that they would not have chosen the book for themselves, initially because they had thought it would be too difficult for them; but they now felt they could get something from it.

PICTURE BOOKS

I also used picture books, which seemed to appeal at all levels. I used them for —

* introducing students to the idea of books being a source of extension of experience and pleasure;
* making the bridge from the classroom to the country being studied;
* allowing the weakest pupils to gain from 'reading the picture'. This is an old method for teaching reading in L1, but is also useful in the modern foreign languages classroom.

To summarise, my programme sought a gradual development in the early years of learning German from —

* the use of sound linked with pictures and graphics, through;
* reading material where the storyline can be moved from almost total reliance on pictures to partial reliance on supporting clues; to
* students able to cope with regulated amounts of unknown materials.

These strategies were employed in order to provide a framework to ensure early progress in cognitive development, and thus enhancing later fluency in reading. In order to bring this latter about I needed to consider ways of encouraging my pupils to engage with longer texts, and to feel more confident about doing so.

Helping pupils to increase their confidence in reading and to tackle more demanding texts

I wanted to encourage pupils to work on their own with texts and, when doing so, to tackle texts that were more demanding. To do this, I realised that I had to provide a framework for shaping their reading habits in German.

WHETTING THEIR APPETITE

Firstly, I read through all the books I had acquired in German with a view to whetting the pupils' appetite to read them. I photocopied paragraphs and pages from the books and set up specific class sessions to look at these.

- I chose explosive passages and short books which could be dramatised within the classroom.

- I selected clips from videos, where I had the corresponding texts. Often the language was not particularly easy, but I wanted mostly to show the pupils aspects of the dramatic possibilities of passages.

At each stage, **discussion was a vital part of the process.** Wherever possible this was carried out in the target language, although English was also used. I felt this was particularly appropriate as my intention was to convey to pupils the excitement to be had from reading. I certainly did not want to intimidate them or scare them by making our discussions nothing more than another linguistic exercise. I tried to move the stages of these discussions from passive to active use of language; from passive to active individual participation.

SOME LIMITATIONS OF THE COMPUTER FOR READING

I explained before how I used storytelling to work at pupils' cognitive learning strategies. I realised that using the computer also would help pupils to match pictures with text. I used a *Fun with Text* package, where the pupils can recognise sentences to make sense after the story has been scrambled. I kept this available for pupils' use. I also decided to keep a set of story-cards available in the library for the pupils to work on producing a re-organised version in place of a computer, should one not be available. My pupils enjoyed using the computer and the success it brought them. Still, I was aware that, as Higgins (1988) notes: '*reading from the screen is a rather different activity from reading from the printed page.*' I agree with him that we enjoy the flexibility of being able to hold the book, or lie it down on a desk, and can frequently remember the shape and colour of the book, if not the author. The computer screen does not have the flexibility we need. My pupils were motivated by it, but I was not satisfied that it was building the sort of literary relations I intended.

VIDEO PLUS TEXT

One of the slightly more difficult books in the library was a book called *Vorstadtkrokodile*. It is the story of a group of children and the gang they form. I found it a delightful story full of lively passages, but rather dry in its published form. Although it had a very colourful cover, it contained a lot of reading material that was uninterrupted by pictures or chapter headings. However, I was able to obtain a video version of it from an exchange link with Germany. I selected a few snippets of action from the tape and the corresponding text was photocopied. We watched the first of the selected pieces without the sound. Appropriate language items such as vocabulary were given to pupils in response to their questions arising from discussion of what they had seen. We also discussed what the students thought would happen next. We then viewed the video again, this time with the sound, and looked at the written text. I felt that by doing so we had experienced many of the aspects a pupil is involved with when reading a story. I recalled:

> '*The act of reading a story involves the reader in picturing, anticipating and retrospecting, interacting and evaluating.*'
> (Benton and Fox, 1985: 13)

I hoped that this would encourage pupils to establish patterns for themselves to follow when reading. I also hoped that they would see that here was a different sort of story for them in the foreign language; but certainly not one outside of their capabilities. I felt that this sort of activity would help pupils to develop their extensive reading by some intensive input.

DISCRETE DIFFERENTIATION

I again considered the use of pictures to help enhance the literary imagination of my pupils in German. I was struck by the research that had been carried out in English language classrooms which suggested that pictures were an excellent way of helping students become less selfconscious about reading. It pointed out that even the most anti-readers often relax with picture books and discuss freely:

> '. . . *whether the words are read aloud or rehearsed in the head, picture book reading tends to be audio-visual. The relative spareness of the words, with their caption-like appearance and their tendency to dialogue, invites the reader to speak them . . . they are sociable, they ask to be shared and may be read by two or three readers of widely differing abilities at once.*'
> (Benton and Fox, 1985: 74)

I felt that this was important. If a choice of picture books are made available for use then each pupil might 'take from the situation' the ability to develop at his or her own pace without it being obvious to another student that they are at a lower or higher stage of development. This **discrete differentiation** seemed to be important to me as teenagers are often very keen to be at one with their peers. Of course, the use of pictures was already standard practice in the publications I was using, such as the *Lesekiste* series and the Mary Glasgow comics. However, I also started to explore the possibilities of pupils developing their own personal picture books.

OLDER LEARNERS PRODUCING A PICTURE BOOK FOR YOUNGER LEARNERS

I asked one of the Year 9 groups of pupils to complete a task of listening to a short story in German and, after a short discussion about the suitability of the storyline, produce a picture book to be used with younger children. This gave rise to some excellent results and most readable products. Where the 'readers' were not effective, the pupils had resorted to too many new words and complicated storylines. The potential reader was offered little support with all this and would have found it overwhelming.

I felt, nevertheless, that this had been a valuable exercise. It recognised many aspects of research on reading; such as the working together of text and picture, the appeal of pictures in the books, the type of script used, etc.

I repeated the exercise with a Year 10 group. With an extra year's maturity, the resulting readers were even better and more professional. With all of these I started to build up a library of materials for use in lessons. With my quest for suitable materials not being an easy one, I felt that this class-produced work was a real step forward.

Establishing pupils' preferences

Even before starting my small piece of action research on developing reading at a pre-GCSE level, it was clear to me that there was an enormous quantity of foreign language material to draw upon. Both magazines and readers seemed to have their place in the classroom, and I believed that pupils should be given a wide choice. I wanted pupils to be able to discriminate between various materials and make choices concerning their own reading. To do this I needed as wide a range of materials as possible. My own work in the area of reader response reminded me of the importance of making various styles available to pupils:

> 'Some of these books will seem worthless, even pernicious, to teachers; but it is arrogant to ignore them and counter-productive to condemn them.' (Benton and Fox, 1985: 61)

But on what basis did pupils make these choices about what they were going to read? Having collected together some 60 books and other material to form the basis of a departmental library, I decided to investigate how my pupils were choosing what to read.

To do this, I conducted a 'get to know the materials' sessions with one Year 10 class of 24 pupils and my Year 9 classes. With both sets I gave them time to browse and then choose a book. Once they had read it, I then conducted a short questionnaire, asking them to complete the statements:

1.   I chose to read this book because . . .
2.   I enjoyed it because . . .
3.(*) I would recommend it to a friend because . . .
      * Year 10 only

The results were as follows:

Students' choices in reading German

Question 1		
Year 10	Year 9	I chose to read it because . . .
2	2	it looked easy to understand
9	8	the cover looked good
6	3	of the cartoon pictures
5	7	of the good pictures inside
3	8	I had already seen the English version and I wanted to see the difference
2	1	it was about someone with my name
2	0	the print looked easy to read
2	1	the characters looked cute
2	1	the text looked simple
2	1	I've seen the film
3	0	it looked different
1	0	I thought that it would give me some ideas
0	1	I chose it in the shop

Year 10	Year 9	**Question 2**
		I enjoyed it because . . .
4	0	it was easy
5	0	it was different
4	0	there were only a few words I didn't know, but I could look them up
5	0	I felt good I could manage some of it
4	1	I read it as a play with a friend
1	0	it was an unusual subject
0	1	I could just read the pictures
1	0	of the good illustrations
2	0	it was fun
1	0	each page was a new story
2	1	it was a bit of a challenge
0	1	I could compare it with my struggle to read English
1	0	I could understand most of it
4	4	I could understand most of it but where I didn't the pictures helped
1	0	I think I met words I wouldn't normally meet in class
1	0	I liked the name for a tadpole
1	0	although it seemed for younger people I still liked it a lot
2	0	it had good descriptions and cute pictures
1	0	it was colourful and attractive and fun to read

Year 10	**Question 3**
	I would recommend it to a friend because . . .
	(only applicable to Year 10)
1	it was easy and short
1	it was funny and about people of our own age group
1	although it wasn't as easy as I thought, it was fun
1	the pictures are good
2	it was different and understandable
2	it was fun
1	it was a bit of a challenge but a good story
1	it was understandable
1	it was simple but effective
4	I enjoyed it
1	I wouldn't, it was too difficult
1	I wouldn't, my friends do not know German

Clearly, these statements reveal much about the attitudes and experiences of my pupils. Their responses open out a whole lot of issues relating to the design and content of foreign language reading materials for secondary school learners.

- For the first statement (Question 1) I was struck by **the importance of visuals**, in particular the front cover, when it came to choosing a book. This seemed to confirm my thoughts about the significance and use of pictures as a support to reading the text.
- I also noticed that many were **attracted by having seen the English language version**. Clearly, there was both curiosity to compare versions, but also knowing something about the story was another support; a way into the text.

Enjoyment of the book was closely connected with having understood it. This is perhaps unsurprising. The negative effects of frustration with struggling to make sense of the texts and the tiredness this causes would have a devastating effect on motivation to read. Again, visuals were important.

The Year 10 replies to why they might recommend the book were quite divergent, as we might expect in such a small group. Two were struck by the novelty of the book, that it was different; two because it was fun; and three because they liked the illustrations.

Conclusion

My study proved to me that it was possible to investigate a particular aspect of my practice with classes. The ideas I had gathered from my studies of the literature on reading had prompted me to discover more about my pupils' attitudes and habits in reading English and foreign language texts. The results I had obtained had enabled me to refine my methodological practice in incorporating reading as a more focused activity in my lessons. In particular, I worked on differentiating intensive and extensive opportunities for reading through a series of strategies. Many had already been around in my arsenal of teaching techniques, but the study provided me with a clearer insight as to what I was aiming for and why. The programme I developed is still in its early stages of implementation, but I am already aware that my pupils have a wider experience of reading than might be the norm in a GCSE classroom.

Eventually, I am hopeful that those pupils who do go on to study German at 'A' level or in the sixth form will find a narrower gulf between GCSE and their new studies than students in the past. If this does come about, it will be because of small changes that make all the difference, and modest objectives reaping richer rewards. It is in this sense that my reflections on practice have led to better practice for me and my pupils.

References

Benton M and G Fox, *Teaching literature 9–14* (Oxford University Press, 1985)

Higgins J, *Language, learners and computers* (Longman, 1988)

Krashen S, *Principles and practice in second language acquisition* (Pergamon, 1982)

Krashen S, *Writing: research, theory and applications* (Pergamon, 1984)

Chapter 2
Reading in French from GCSE to 'A' level: the student perspective

by Patricia Rees

Reading plays a key part in learning, using, teaching and examining a foreign language, and increasingly so as the student climbs the educational ladder. The problems that students face daily in the classroom when reading in a language other than their first language raise intriguing and challenging issues such as the nature of the reading process and the importance of reading skills.

In my teaching I have been concerned with students moving from 'O' level — latterly from GCSE — to 'A' level French. There have also been readers in a hurry, who, deciding against 'A' level French, have nevertheless needed to decipher written text requiring a competence greater than attained in 'O' level or GCSE — for example, candidates for the French Reading Comprehension Paper of the JMB's General Studies 'A' level. How best to help them, given the little extra teaching time allocated, further focused my thoughts on the problems of the foreign language reader.

COMMUNICATION STUDIES GROUP: L1 AND L2

I was enabled to develop this interest during a part-time MA in Education (Language, Literature and Media Studies) at Southampton University from 1987 to 1990, with a half-day secondment from Hampshire County Council. Interaction with members of a Communication Studies group, mostly teachers of English as a First Language with a smaller number of MFL teachers, posed the question of how far difficulties in deciphering text were reading difficulties *per se* or foreign sociolinguistic and psycholinguistic factors involved in the reading process. Major theoretical influences on my MA (Ed) dissertation were *Understanding reading — a psycholinguistic analysis of reading and learning to read* (Smith, 1982), *Developing reading skills* (Grellet, 1981) and *Teaching reading skills in a foreign language* (Nuttall, 1982).

This chapter, which grew out of my MA (Ed), reports on practical research which I carried out in 1990 among first-year 'A' level English students of French at a Hampshire sixth form college. It offers a profile of their experience as readers of French as they progress from GCSE to 'A' level, and examines a number of issues highlighted by the fieldwork findings, together with their implications for the classroom.

THE STUDENTS

The students concerned were the 1989 entry, the second intake of 'A' level students with a GCSE background. The organisation of secondary education in Hampshire, with virtually county-wide eleven–sixteen or twelve–sixteen secondary schools followed by sixteen–nineteen secondary or sixth form colleges, means that students at the colleges come from a diversity of secondary schools with many different French teachers, for whom the GCSE is an end point. There is no built-in continuity of teaching, such as is found in a 'straight-through' eleven–nineteen or twelve–nineteen institution, though there is liaison between secondary schools and secondary colleges.

MY AIMS

My aims were multiple. I wanted to find out what our new students had actually read in French before GCSE, their reactions to this, and how they experienced the transition to 'A' level as readers of French. Moreover, it seemed useful to compare theory with practice.

- What could we learn directly from the students, unfiltered through teachers' perceptions or documents, about the interface between GCSE and 'A' level French?
- How did their experience connect with the requirements of the examination boards?
- How could we best help them and their successors to read in a foreign language? I was therefore interested in their experience of study skills and reading strategies.

TAKING SOUNDINGS

Soundings were taken concerning three stages in the development of a year-group of 'A' level French students:

- first, retrospectively, with reference to GCSE;
- second, to the point of transition at the start of the 'A' level course;
- third, with reference to the (then) present, at the end of the first year of this course.

These soundings were conducted by means of a questionnaire and group interviews.

SYLLABUS A AND SYLLABUS B GROUPS

The students surveyed came from four sets with three teachers. For historical reasons they were following two separate 'A' level syllabuses, each having different reading requirements in French. One set was studying for the London A syllabus, with a literature paper on three set texts taken from a list prescribed by the board and a reading comprehension paper. The other three sets were preparing for the SUJB/Cambridge syllabus B, with neither a literature nor a reading comprehension paper, but incorporating an individual study and an extensive reading programme. The individual study dealt with an aspect of French life and culture, chosen by the students themselves but requiring approval by the board. This necessitated the reading of documents and/or books in French which might be but would probably not be creative literature. The reading programme of approximately ten books in French, chosen by staff and students, was examined at the oral as a discussion topic only.

PHASE ONE: QUESTIONNAIRE STUDY

The questionnaire, my first small-scale study, was designed to find out as much as possible from the students about their experience of reading in French before they entered the college at 16+. I wanted their perception of events.

Fifty questionnaires were distributed to first-year 'A' level students in early July at the end of the third term of their course. Thirty-five were completed by respondents who had attended eleven different contributory secondary schools and who had had at least as many different teachers between them.

THE PLACE OF READING

As a starting point I wanted to ascertain how the students had perceived the relative importance of **reading** French in their secondary schools, bearing in mind that all four communicative skills — listening, speaking, reading and writing — are weighted equally at GCSE, each being allocated 25% of the total mark.

It emerged that, viewed from the students' perspective:

• the front runner by far in the hierarchy of skills was writing;
• reading had occupied second place;
• closely followed by listening;
• with speaking last.

What students had read

The questions on reading materials were broken down into sub-sections on coursebooks, past papers, photocopied texts, magazines and newspapers, readers in French, books in French (complete books as distinct from readers or books of extracts) and French poetry.

COURSEBOOKS

I found that coursebooks had filled the foreground of the students' French reading experience. *Tricolore* predominated, with 24 users. Fewer than five had used any other. A small proportion had used ancillary books based on one or more discrete communicative skills alongside or instead, with an even tinier proportion using more than one.

PAST PAPERS

Past papers are very special animals, being by definition a medium for testing. They are specially selected and often doctored to that end. Of the 26 students who had used past papers to practise reading comprehension skills in French, twelve had used between four and five of them. This is probably an adequate number to prepare for the examination if used **alongside** other reading materials.

Six students denied using past papers, and a further three did not know or were not sure, so nine of the 35 could not say they **had** used them, about one quarter of the total. It is doubtful if this is adequate preparation for the examination room, but at the other extreme the two students who worked on fifteen and twenty past papers respectively may well have suffered from a chronic surfeit of a limited diet of text and question types.

PHOTOCOPIED TEXTS

Photocopied texts or passages for reading in French had been used by 27 respondents. Twenty-one had found them useful; about half (fourteen) had enjoyed them. A common thread in responses was that they offered a welcome variety in terms of relevance, topics, styles and vocabulary extending beyond coursebooks.

MAGAZINES AND NEWSPAPERS

Only six students claimed to have read any magazines or newspapers in French. Only three could supply any names — mostly of purpose-built products from educational publishing houses.

READERS IN FRENCH

Several students did not know the term 'reader' and requested clarification. Nine out of the 35 students were certain that they had used readers, which suggests that up to 26 had not. Surprisingly, eight readers had been used during class time, while only three had been used for private study or homework, despite their suitability for these purposes. Perhaps the reason was a shortage of books, or a fear that they would be lost if taken home.

The nine students' overall impressions of their readers came across as very favourable, not only because they felt them to have been an extension of their reading skills but also because they perceived them as confidence-boosters, providing confirmation of skills already acquired.

COMPLETE BOOKS IN FRENCH

The readership of 'complete books' in French other than readers had been extremely low. Only three out of 35 students had read any, and then only one apiece. They were estimated by them to be between 100 and 287 pages in length, with two of the three students reading them to the end. All found them useful, while two out of the three found them enjoyable — the ones who also finished them!

FRENCH POETRY

Six of the 35 students had read a very small amount of poetry. Only La Fontaine and Prévert were named. All enjoyed the poems they read, explaining why eloquently. This was unexpected, in view of the widespread belief that poetry fails to fire the modern sixteen-year-old, but there seems to be a rich vein of personal fulfilment to be tapped through this genre of imaginative writing, if texts are well chosen.

TEXT LENGTH

The respondents' experience of text length proved highly revealing. GCSE coursebook texts mirror texts in GCSE reading tests in length. Aside from the three students who had tackled whole books of up to 287 pages, the single student who had read a magazine of 50 pages, the three who had read similar materials of about twenty pages and the handful who had read readers of about 25 pages — and some of the students came within more than one of these categories — a clear majority of these post-GCSE students had read nothing longer than, at best, four or five paragraphs of continuous text in French. Two to three paragraphs had been more usual. Thus their experience had not exceeded the length of the reading comprehension questions in the GCSE examination papers. Unsurprisingly, therefore, students continuing on to 'A' level courses find the longer texts there difficult to handle.

Students were asked whether they had received any kind of reading skills training in their secondary schools. Five students, one seventh of the sample, claimed to have followed a reading skills course. In no case had it been linked with French. It had formed part of normal lessons in English or History; four of the five had found it helpful.

Students were also asked about the role played by their French teacher in providing advice on tackling reading assignments in French. Only one fifth of them could recall specific advice.

They were asked too whether their coursebooks had contained hints on reading strategies and, if so, whether these hints had been useful. Four only, one in nine, recalled advice in coursebooks, but only one of the four could name this advice.

In response to a direct question 22 of our 35 respondents said they would have welcomed a reading skills course in French; eleven did not reply; some gave as their reason that they would then be more effective as readers of French at 'A' level.

GUIDANCE ON READING FROM THE BOARDS

A syllabus is a public document. Students were questioned on their access to their boards' French syllabus and on their awareness of advice from the boards on tackling the examination.

The NEA French syllabus is distinctive in printing extensive advice on reading skills in French (Section 6, 'Communication strategies': 29–33). Although not actually advocating that the 'Communication strategies' section of the syllabus should be placed in the students' hands in its neat form, the board nevertheless expects them to be familiar enough with its contents to apply them to language in context:

> *'Candidates cannot be expected to have met and mastered all the linguistic elements they will meet when reading and listening to authentic French. This leads to the need to develop communication strategies that can be used to cope successfully with unknown words. . . These strategies will greatly increase the candidates' ability to cope when they meet, or need, language which they have not previously met or have forgotten.'* (29)

Recommended strategies included:

- ignoring words not needed for successful completion of the task set;
- using the visual and verbal context, grammatical markers and categories, social and cultural context and common elements which English shares with French such as prefixes and suffixes;

- recognising and understanding characteristic noun endings, diminutives, etc, cognates and near-cognates. A list of 23 rules also helps in understanding thousands of words in French which are neither cognates nor near-cognates.

Had therefore the 23 out of 35 respondents who had taken the NEA French papers at GCSE become acquainted with these hints, either through self-study or via the teacher?

Although fourteen said they had seen a copy of the board's syllabus, only one claimed to have read and found useful the hints on reading skills printed there. The possibility exists of defective recall. Maybe, too, this advice was conveyed to the students indirectly or in diluted form within the classroom only as they applied to individual texts. The fact remains that the students had not been conscious of assistance from the examination board in this respect.

PHASE TWO: THE FOLLOW-UP INTERVIEWS

The questionnaire provided a profile of the respondents' reading in French before they took their GCSE at 16+ and left their secondary schools. It established that the vast majority of them had never read texts consisting of more than three paragraphs of continuous prose nor any imaginative writing in French.

With this profile, how did these students fare at the start of their 'A' level course as readers of French? I wanted to try to identify how they had perceived this activity —

- both at the point of entry to the college;
- and at the end of the first year of their 'A' level course in July.

My second small-scale study consisted of follow-up group interviews.

FLEXIBILITY OF THE INTERVIEW

The interview was chosen for its flexibility. I could go on a 'fishing' expedition, to borrow the analogy coined by Wiseman and Aron, and could 'put flesh on the bones of questionnaire responses' (Bell, 1987: 70) through following up points made, picking up cues and probing replies. I wanted a group dynamic, to let the students bounce ideas off each other, to let thought associations flow. Also, it would be reassuring after the highly structured and fairly lengthy questionnaire. Our dialogues were less like interviews than informal conversations on tape, part way along what Gebenek and Moser term 'a continuum of formality' (Bell, 1987: 71).

RECORDING THE INTERVIEWS

I opted for recording for several reasons:

- to obtain a complete record of what the students said and of the interplay between us all;
- to capture their tone of voice;
- to follow and take part in the dialogue myself as required, without the constraint of taking notes.

We sat informally round a table, on which a cassette recorder was placed and left to run throughout. The total length of the recordings was about one and a half hours.

The interviews took place during the third week of July, about ten days after the questionnaire had been completed, the timing providing a space for further thoughts and even afterthoughts. A day or so in advance I outlined the areas for discussion, but I did not ask participants to prepare their answers. I repeated these explanations just before the interviews.

INTERVIEW QUESTIONS

I worked from a sheet of rough notes giving the areas to be covered, opening the dialogue with:

- Now that you have had a year on the 'A' level course, how do you feel about reading in French? Please would you describe your experience.

Though unscripted, the questions covered the following aspects:

- How did you feel at first (at the beginning of the year)? What problems were there, if any?
- How do you now feel after a year?
- How do you feel as you look ahead to next year?
- What could we do to help you with any problems?
- What would you like to see in a reading course?

WHO WERE THE INTERVIEWEES?

The eleven participants, just over one fifth of the year group, were all volunteers from among the respondents to the questionnaire. They had attended eight different contributory schools, seven state and one private sector. Three were from syllabus A and eight from syllabus B, proportions closely reflecting those on the two French courses. However, males were slightly over-represented among the interviewees.

The three syllabus A students were interviewed together in one group, while the syllabus B students were divided into three different groups. I wished to find out whether the syllabus chosen had had any marked effect on their first year as 'A' level readers of French.

To preserve anonymity I have given the students invented first names according to their sex. Their comments are actual quotations transcribed from the tape.

Analysis of group discussions: the syllabus A students

There was consensus that the early weeks, even months, of the transition were a shock. The growing pains were particularly acute for the three studying for the 'A' level with literature. All syllabus A students had chosen this freely out of an interest in literature. Typical comments were:

> 'We didn't do much reading at GCSE at my last school so I found it quite difficult at 'A' level. It was a really big change.' (Mary)

> 'It was a huge jump.' (Jane)

> 'I don't think I was given anything to read, about half a page perhaps, newspaper articles about tourist attractions in the South of France, things like that, things which were relevant to GCSE.' (Jane)

> 'Yes. They actually said, didn't they, that, you know, that they were just going to give you what you needed to pass the GCSE and nothing more really . . . and GCSE's just so different to 'A' level.' (Mary)

The new [transitional] coursebook, *Orientations* (1985), at the start of the college year had proved 'something of a shock', despite its careful selection by their teachers as a bridging text. The students focused on vocabulary, reading speed and text length.

VOCABULARY

Peter commented:

> 'We were presented with this book full of new vocabulary . . . something which we hadn't really been used to up until then.'

and added reflectively:

> 'But the more you actually take in of vocabulary, the more you can cope with other reading material . . . in the end, you can only benefit, can't you?'

Mary, who found problems with structures and vocabulary, *'everything really'*, appreciated the coursebook for having the vocabulary on the page:

> *'because if you're reading something and then you have to go and look a word up, then you forget what you were reading anyway by the time you've found it and it just sort of seems like, you know, thousands of words that you just keep translating. It doesn't seem like it's building up and making anything.'*

TEXT LENGTH

This group's discussion of reading was dominated by the problem of coping with *Elise ou la vraie vie* by Claire Etcherelli. The choice of texts was subject to book cupboard constraints and prescription by the board. This novel was chosen first, in preference to the other two available prescribed books, Anouilh's *L'alouette* and Maupassant's *Boule de suif*. We hoped it would prove more relevant and immediate for them because of its relatively contemporary theme. Its start was delayed until the spring term, on grounds that it would have been too difficult to tackle in the autumn.

All three students agreed that they couldn't have begun to cope with reading a whole book in their first month in college. As Jane put it, pleased, nevertheless, with her progress:

> *'You move from reading a paragraph, which is about five lines in GCSE, and then in a year you're having to read a book, which you don't think is possible at the beginning of the year. At the end of the year you think, 'I don't know how I've done it.'*

TRANSLATION

The students themselves raised the issue of translation versus reading comprehension as a means of tackling their set text, commenting on their difficulties in reading it, but disagreeing among themselves over whether it should be translated. In class they had earlier bewailed the current unavailability of an out-of-print English translation. They would have liked to study them side by side. Peter and Mary (who admitted to translating as she read) wanted to translate it all; Jane felt there was not time for this, admitting frankly that she didn't look forward to reading it because:

> *'a page takes about half-an-hour to read in French.'*

Mary, who really liked *Elise,* found it:

> '*so difficult to read at home on my own because it just takes so long . . . in places I just get really lost if we don't translate it bit by bit.*'

They all regretted the absence of vocabulary at the back of the book.

CULTURAL CONTEXT

Jane observed that the notes after the text were very welcome because they explained cultural features that, not being French, they wouldn't know about otherwise.

LOOKING BACK ON THE YEAR

All agreed that after one year problems of vocabulary, structure, and cultural differences remained. Jane said that she and other students had found the transition between GCSE and 'A' level much harder than with English:

> '*English 'A' level is more, sort of, a continuation of GCSE, whereas French 'A' level is completely different to French GCSE . . . , it's like a transition from reading something like playschool books to something like Thomas Hardy.*'

and

> '*It's like jumping into a huge river when it should have been a stream.*'

All three felt more confident in relation to reading in French after a year, two with reservations. Mary added:

> '*You don't learn anything at all about the foundations in GCSE. I think they missed that bit out.*'

EASING THE TRANSITION

The group was fertile in ideas about how to ease the transition from GCSE to 'A' level in relation to reading:

> '*As soon as you come in, you could start off with an* Easy Reader *(e.g. a 'baby' Simenon).*' (Peter)

> '*Something which is perhaps designed for a French child of perhaps eleven or twelve, something like that.*' (Jane)

> '*Something that you get the satisfaction of saying, 'I've read a*

book in French', *even though it's not a particularly good book in French.'* (Jane)

VALUE OF GRAMMAR AND TRANSLATION

The students were unclear what a 'reading course' entailed:

- Jane felt she needed grammar before reading; she didn't know how it could be done.
- All three students wanted to read the text in translation (a controversial aspect of language teaching policy).

The point of reading the book in translation first was: to get the main idea (Peter); so as not to get the wrong idea and go off at a tangent (Jane and Mary). Mary, who would have liked to work with the text and the translation side by side, also, interestingly, reasoned:

'so that I can see how the sentences are constructed, how they work out.'

that is, for syntactical, language-learning reasons too.

OTHER AIDS TO READING

Discussion then centred on other aids to reading:

- Jane said that perhaps what they needed was, *'just a paragraph for each chapter, saying roughly what's happened, something like that.'*
- Mary suggested a paragraph in simpler French, just giving the main ideas. They agreed that they meant a reading key or, instead, a summary of the theme.

I proposed a reader's guide, with questions on the text serving as signposts, so that the students would know they were going to cross a certain kind of terrain but would have to identify the actual landmarks for themselves. Only Jane felt she would be unable to arrive at the answers by this means. Mary added:

'Yes. You need something to make you focus on certain points of the book . . . otherwise . . . it goes over your head . . . if you look at certain bits in more detail, you understand it better and take more in.'

All three agreed their set book would be easier when revising in term 5 than in terms 2 and 3 because they would know more structures by then.

FORMAT OF THE SET TEXT

The format of the set text was discussed:

• They liked the idea of a layout with vocabulary on the page itself, as with their coursebook.
• They felt too it would be helpful to have structures picked out beside the text. This would spoil the story less than looking them up themselves elsewhere.

USEFUL READING STRATEGIES

On the question of a reading skills course, and with reference to strategies used by their 'A' level teacher:

• two students found help with *faux amis* useful;
• though the third thought it made her over-cautious;
• they agreed that they looked for key words when reading.

Also considered useful were:

• looking at word roots;
• the use of prefixes;
• breaking words down into their component parts, though somewhat curiously the only student to have done any Latin felt it had never helped.

Such activities seemed new to them after their GCSE, although they feature prominently in the 'Communication strategies' section of the NEA syllabus.

Analysis of group discussions: the syllabus B students

In this account I have conflated groups 2, 3 and 4 consisting of eight students in all. These students, with an individual study and a reading programme examined at the oral, agonised less over the adaptation to 'A' level reading than those with prescribed literature texts, but still felt, in Mark's words, that:

> 'In general terms the actual gap between GCSE and 'A' level is quite large.'

All owned up to difficulties with the length of texts and the quantity of new vocabulary. They summed up their feelings as follows:

> 'GCSE doesn't prepare you at all.' (Susan)

> 'Reading is so important for 'A' level. Such an important part of the course.' (Luke)

TEXT LENGTH

Students spoke feelingly about their previous experience of text length:

> *'Just little paragraphs, about two paragraphs long. Now we do whole books . . . we do the whole story.'* (Ann)

Apart from her coursebook, Carol had only read comic books at GCSE with very simple vocabulary. Mark, whose reading experience had only been through textbook exercises, thought at first:

> *'the idea of reading literature was a bit frightening in some ways, but now that we've done some and sort of over the year getting introduced to it slowly, the idea of doing it is not such a problem any more.'*

VOCABULARY

All noted the volume of new vocabulary that came with 'A' level. John found most daunting all the consultations of the dictionary which were now necessary; the problem would have been even greater with a different textbook. They were grateful for having vocabulary on the page in *Orientations* (1985).

John was preoccupied with idiomatic French, which he found difficult. He felt that he had been kept away from idiom at GCSE. Others picked up on this: the language at GCSE, they felt, didn't go beyond how to handle practical situations, and had been lacking in images as well as idioms.

Susan pinpointed the transition in relation to *Orientations*: she found coping with its vocabulary a shock, despite certain similarities to her previous GCSE textbook. Texts were longer and the vocabulary much more extensive. On starting 'A' level she knew hardly any vocabulary. Her GCSE class hadn't read any book or poems.

SUBJECT MATTER

Carol found *Orientations* unfamiliar at first; she quite liked it, however, because of its contemporary texts. In general, the students regarded it as a good transition. They liked the serial, *Une Française d'aujourd'hui,* which, as Mark put it, *'eased you into new things'.* John said it was:

> *'corny, but fun because of that and you could go through it progressively; there were lots of useful idiomatic sentences in it.'*

Carol was pleased that topics were now more controversial, while John was delighted that they were more profound and wider-ranging, with themes such as nature, animals and conservation.

UNDERSTANDING THE TEXT

Another new aspect for Mark was forming opinions about the French text. Working out what the author was trying to say was quite difficult to start with, but that seemed to be better now. Gordon also referred to his difficulties, his:

> 'uncertainty how to pronounce things, what things meant and how the sentences went together, how you were supposed to read them together . . . to make something that was sensible, so you would guess . . . I got very thrown by the structures and you get very confused by the way they were worded, and you'd end up with the wrong meaning.'

It had been a matter of reducing and eliminating the guesswork. He had found that the most helpful thing had been his teacher:

> 'just talking us through the difficulties.'

Structures had not appeared to create many problems for syllabus B students, however. I pointed out that *Orientations* did ease you into this aspect of the course, while simultaneously introducing much new vocabulary. The group that had read Roger Vailland's *325000 francs* as the first book on their reading programme, starting in the spring, felt it would have been impossible at the beginning of the first term. Carol stated that not having learnt the past historic yet would have been quite confusing. Susan's alarm on first having the Vailland novel in her hands had abated. Gordon wouldn't have been able to cope with his first whole book in French, *L'étranger* by Camus, at the start of term 1, but felt much happier with reading in French after a year:

> 'I'm not so worried about it now, so that I can enjoy it and I can learn things from it as well . . . it's quite satisfying to be able to read a magazine and to know that you can actually understand what they are writing about, to understand perhaps a current affairs issue or something and it's about France and that you wouldn't hear in England and you can understand it from a French magazine.'

WHICH SYLLABUS?

Mark had opted for the syllabus without a literature paper, wanting French for everyday situations in the French-speaking world. He was also more interested in learning about life in France than analysing books and their writers. Four students were adamant that they had chosen the 'A' level without literature because their syllabus, the 'B' is more 'relevant' nowadays. Carol felt too that with this syllabus:

*'it's more reading for pleasure. You can choose what sort of
area interests you.'*

These B syllabus students, certain they had progressed, now had no qualms
about tackling their reading programme. Mark said:

*'We've been given an insight into what we're going to be doing
for our reading programme. having learned so much vocabulary
over the first year, it will be a lot easier to read the books.'*

John thought that the book had expanded not only his vocabulary but also his
understanding of grammar which he had had difficulty in learning in a set lesson,
finding it easier to grasp in the context of a story. Carol felt that although there
are more structures and vocabulary to cope with than before, *'It will come as I
go along'*. Gordon said:

*'So far on the reading side I think I've had a good foundation . . .
to carry on to do the rest of the books [the reading programme]
I've got to do and to carry on learning.'*

EASING THE TRANSITION

All three in one group found the reader they had been given earlier in the year
helpful. It was a simplified version of a Simenon story taken from an old 'O' level
book cupboard. Should they have had such a book for GCSE? They said that it
could perhaps have provided some psychological benefit, but was not needed for
GCSE itself.

Carol voiced the view that reading problems came from the way that GCSE was
taught. Their ideas on assistance with reading included:

- giving prior insight into the nature of the subject (Mark);
- long articles (Gordon);
- vocabulary on the same page as the text (several students) and;
- a little story, an easy reader with a vocabulary at the back to start with
  (unanimous recommendation).

They liked discussion to make sure they had understood. One student praised
from personal experience a simplified version of Maupassant short stories in the
Textes en français facile (TFF) series.

Sixth form teachers would strongly endorse Gordon's comment that anyone
starting 'A' level French should keep the reading going once GCSE is over, and
read something in French, anything, in the holidays.

Brief and fairly unfocused discussions of a potential reading course encompassed:

- hints on how to read effectively;
- introductory pointers for reading a book (Carol);
- *'cracking words up into bits'* (John);
- the need for study aids such as a good dictionary;
- reading chiefly non-fictional materials on current affairs and similar topics.

Four students wanted:

- more long(er) extracts from magazines and papers from France and Belgium and;
- texts on controversies as recent as the previous week.

Three of the four advocated:

- more plays in class, each taking parts.

They were avid for:

- a wide variety of subject matter and styles.

Language awareness activities such as the above-mentioned 'word cracking' were also considered. One student remembered having done some at the college in class, but another from the same group could not recall this and asked what it was. Gordon had noticed that it could be helpful to look at words and work them out by the way they are made up.

Other forms of vocabulary acquisition were also discussed. Susan thought vocabulary tests make you learn it. Might there be other ways of retaining vocabulary? Martin and Luke felt that because you enjoy doing 'A' level, which is a two-year course, some of it recurs anyway, and also, as Luke put it:

'you learn it because you want to speak the language and be coherent in the language and to have the vocabulary to do it.'

A synthesis of my findings

WHAT READING IN FRENCH MEANT TO STUDENTS

The questionnaire and the interviews showed that at the end of their first 'A' level year, and after reflecting together on the reading process, our students knew what reading in French now meant to them:

How can the students help us? What I learnt from them

Listening to the students talking about their perceptions as learners confronting written texts and reading their comments on the questionnaires afforded me many valuable insights. I felt that the experience was a learning process for all concerned.

I was delighted by the students' willingness to participate in this research and to communicate their views. They knew from the brief they were given that the purpose was to help them and their successors identify and overcome problems in reading in a foreign language. This seemed to be very motivating for them.

REFLECTION AS A LEARNING EXPERIENCE

I was impressed by the relaxed manner, the fluent responses and the reflectiveness of the interviewees as they sat around the tape recorder. These qualities speak for themselves in the written and recorded statements that I have quoted.

Both during and looking back on the interviews, I had, too, a strong sense that the process of thinking about and discussing their reading that we had gone through together had not only yielded information of use in teaching, but had also in itself served as a learning experience. As well as being an exercise in greater self-awareness, **it played a developmental role in their language awareness.** In taking stock the students acquired insights and became conscious of having done so. They knew at the end of the year's 'A' level work what the process of reading in a foreign language now meant to them; they also had a very clear idea of what their needs were, as indeed of the constraints imposed by their examination syllabuses.

INCREASED EMPATHY: A DIALOGUE OF DISCOVERY

I certainly acquired far more empathy with my students' problems with reading. One instance of this is the seemingly mountainous hurdle of masses of unknown vocabulary. We know of these problems in principle. However, in teaching, intellectual awareness of students' areas of difficulty does not seem to me to be knowledge of the same order as being helped to see their problems through their own eyes. This is one of the great gains that I made during my research.

This dialogue of discovery between teacher and learner can be conducted individually, though there is a risk that shyness could prove a barrier with some, whereas others thrive on a one-to-one contact. However, small groups may sometimes be more productive since there is the element of reporting on shared experience, and solidarity can be a form of reinforcement. Moreover, while profiling, essentially an individual contact with the teacher, may help to meet this need and certainly should result in greater student self-awareness, its very context as part of an appraisal system makes it difficult for a judgemental element to be excluded and for genuine informality to be achieved.

VALUE OF TIME-OUT SESSIONS

I would therefore make a plea for 'time out' sessions such as I was able to experience as part of this research, so that teachers can engage in informal dialogue with their students and reflect together on the learning process. Unfortunately with the current proliferation of other tasks: administration, changes in syllabuses and testing, growing pastoral needs, to give but some, reflection on practice, including discussion with colleagues, is increasingly taking a back seat.

How can we help the students? Some recommendations

The results of my enquiries among the students lead me towards certain recommendations. These are based extensively on their needs as readers as well as on my own previous theoretical reading.

A STRUCTURED READING PROGRAMME

My research strengthened my belief in the importance of a programme of structured intensive and extensive reading in the foreign language classroom, both pre- and post-16.

There should be preliminary transitional work on reading skills incorporating close, or intensive, reading of short(er) texts followed by increasingly extensive reading.

This programme should address the following issues which will be considered below:

- range
- relevance
- text length
- vocabulary and syntax
- layout
- reading purposes and outcomes
- general context
- cultural context
- reading skills training
- reading strategies
- extensive and intensive reading
- the place of readers
- reinforcement.

A RANGE OF MATERIALS

During the very early stages of the 'A' level course a wide variety of text types is necessary, to provide stimulus and intellectual challenge, and a broad experience of themes, style and vocabulary.

RELEVANCE OF THE SUBJECT MATTER

Reading is an individual and sometimes lonely activity. Relevance is a strong motivator, a powerful stimulus to reading. This was stressed in the questionnaire responses. For the foreign language reader who has to strive that much harder, perceived relevance will be even more desirable. We should try to meet the students' demand for relevant reading materials as far as possible, even more so in their personal reading.

LENGTH OF TEXT

A staged progression in text length is important. Texts should gradually be lengthened from the habitual two to three paragraphs of GCSE to a whole page, thence to two or three pages, then five to ten, then mini-books or readers, and finally 'whole' books.

VOCABULARY AND SYNTAX

A staged progression in exposure to more demanding vocabulary and structures is also desirable in the early months of the post-GCSE course, starting at or just beyond the level of difficulty experienced at GCSE, bearing in mind that students are rusty after the long summer break.

LAYOUT

This is crucial for readability. In my students' experience, having vocabulary and structures picked out on the page and explained in a wide margin beside the text is a valuable reading aid. A visually attractive page is also motivating.

SHARING OBJECTIVES

My research strengthened my belief in the educational importance of sharing our **mutual** objectives with the learners. Maybe we sometimes take it for granted that they understand the point of their activities.

SHARING REASONS FOR READING

Students should know **broadly why** they are reading a given text, unless it is planned as a mystery tour or as a test. Explaining to them in advance why it is important assists motivation and also supplies context.

FIXING OUTCOMES

Our students also need specific reading outcomes which they keep in mind or have at their elbow as they embark on the text. Tasks known in advance to the student, such as quizzes, written exploitation or individual or group oral work, help to provide focus and a clear reading purpose.

These 'props' of known purposes and outcomes are especially vital at the earlier stages of training. They can gradually be reduced or removed as skills develop and reader autonomy increases.

GENERAL CONTEXTUALISATION

Landmarks are needed. The length and nature of the text will dictate which type of assistance is most appropriate. These landmarks could be pointers of highlights, strategic breaks in the text, a reader's guide with structured questions, explanatory paragraphs on each chapter, or summaries. Known outcomes also serve as landmarks.

CULTURAL CONTEXT

Publishers should provide more cultural background in an introduction or in note form, e.g. at the back of a text. Our students wanted this as a crucial element in understanding the text and out of general educational interest. It is useful for staff too.

READING SKILLS TRAINING

The questionnaire showed that, as far as they could recall, the 'A' level students surveyed had scarcely experienced this type of training and therefore their suggestions remained fairly vague. Not one made specific mention of help with reading speed in any language or in other subjects.

READING STRATEGIES

Reading skills strategies will need to be tackled early in the 'A' level course. Students should be trained in effective 'text-attack' skills (Grellet, 1981; Nuttall, 1982). This aggressive term signals that the reader's role is **active.** Both learner and teacher must acknowledge this if effective reading is to occur.

Without unduly burdening the students, we should also share with them the hints on reading and other study strategies issued by examination boards. At 16+ we could use or revise advice such as 'Communication strategies' in Section 6 of the NEA GCSE French syllabus. As my survey showed, prior to GCSE disappointingly little use had apparently been made of this material, even though it underpins the marking scheme for the NEA GCSE reading papers, notably at higher level.

This advice needs, however, to be communicated in a form accessible to a range of learners, so it will not always be realistic to administer it neat, using lists of 'rules'. Though some students may be able to absorb and digest it in this guise, for most it will be too abstract and will require interpretation. Concrete examples will need to be recognised in context, within a text. Conversely, if we teach the particular without the general, we deprive students of the opportunity and capacity to transfer this knowledge to other situations to which it applies. Understanding the meaning of prefixes in known words and being able to apply them to new words would be a case in point.

The students' observations revealed the increase in their language awareness since GCSE. Yet they were unable to provide many suggestions in this area without some prompting from me. Their divided views on whether vocabulary tests aid vocabulary retention perhaps reflect current disagreement on policy among teachers and the time-consuming nature of constant testing. The response was also mixed concerning the various devices for vocabulary building that came into the discussion, all of which had been used by their 'A' level teachers, though not usually as a systematic exercise: recognition of cognates and *faux amis*, looking at word roots and families, understanding of prefixes, for example.

From my own experience I remain convinced of the importance of the reading strategies discussed above for the advanced English-speaking reader of French as a foreign language. Ways and means of inculcating them do seem to me, though, to demand further empirical, as well as theoretical, investigation. Indeed, should training in transferable skills not perhaps already have begun with mother tongue teaching at a previous stage in the educational cycle?

INTENSIVE AND EXTENSIVE READING

My findings concerning our two sets of students support the concept of an extensive reading programme as against the intensive study of a very few 'set texts'. I was led to conclude, however, that such a programme will be implemented most effectively only after the preliminary transitional work on reading skills incorporating close, or intensive, reading of short(er) texts outlined above.

It is intensive reading that makes the greatest demands on the student. I am dubious whether it is desirable for the majority of sixteen- to nineteen-year-old students to study long(er) set literature texts in the FL **for the purposes of literary criticism.** This form of **extensive reading** comprising the literary analysis of a long text shades into a lengthy form of **intensive reading.**

Because of the students' limited linguistic knowledge at this stage, the task of deciphering the text is long, drawn-out and laborious. Certainly helping the students to decode the text before it could be discussed as literature monopolised a disproportionate amount of classroom time and meant we had less to spend on other language activities. Moreover, too many skills are called into play at once. Detail and close focus are required as well as gist comprehension. The skills of literary judgement are also entailed. And the final lap of this marathon is an examination paper which also incorporates a memory test.

Should examination boards only set texts at sixteen- to nineteen-year-old level if available editions take account of students' reading age in the foreign language?

Our A syllabus students would have answered this in the affirmative. They deplored the fact that boards could set texts when the only readily available editions offered either scant or no help with the vocabulary. The subject matter was appropriate to their level of emotional maturity, but the assumed level of vocabulary acquisition was more undergraduate, so that notes only covered the most obscure expressions.

Although assistance was automatically given in class with deciphering the text, the students also wanted greater facilities for self-study and revision. They had access to good dictionaries, but as we have seen from their response to the survey, and as their teachers would confirm, looking up most words on a page in a large dictionary throughout a lengthy text is exceedingly discouraging and sometimes demotivating.

THE PLACE OF READERS

Readers have an important bridging role. They fulfil a useful function, early in the course, but not right at the outset. They represent a reassuring halfway house between the snippet, the short text and the daunting full-length or 'whole' book. They also foster reader autonomy.

Readers were positively liked by those students to whom they had been issued, and were unanimously recommended by my respondents. In most cases they had formed no part of their pre-16+ experience.

Some of the former 'O' level readers may still be lurking in stock cupboards. They may not be too superannuated. Provided their readability is high and they are appropriate to the age, aptitude and tastes of the learner, they can be dusted down and brought out again.

Ideally readers should not be 'cooked' script, manufactured expressly for language-teaching purposes, but authentic texts, simplified perhaps, and graduated according to difficulty and the number of words. There should be landmarks here too to guide the reader: simple, preferably monolingual, notes giving linguistic definitions and cultural explanations, together with the support of glossaries, reader's guides and other study aids.

265–9). Some CALL software was pressed into service to facilitate interactive reading comprehension and vocabulary expansion via language games.

What lies ahead?

In 1990 our 'A' level students perceived the discontinuity between GCSE and 'A' level curricula in French. They identified for themselves the transactional nature of the language and activities which predominated in the GCSE work. At this point in their development as linguists they deemed it insufficient. They were not asked in the survey whether they had already felt this in secondary school, and much of this realisation probably came with hindsight, after exposure to different linguistic demands, registers, perspectives, and materials on their post-16 courses.

At all events our students' comments reveal a sense that their GCSE French was strongly flavoured with utilitarianism, and not only in relation to its transactional characteristics, but also because of syllabus requirements — things had not been covered because they were not 'needed' for GCSE. Is this simply the fate of all closely defined syllabuses, indeed of all syllabuses, in the real world?

Again this was a retrospective judgement. But it unerringly highlights the nature of the difficulties that staff and students faced with the introduction of GCSE. 'A' level had followed on smoothly from the former 'O' level, whatever the latter's faults. In 1990 our students discovered for themselves the mismatch (which still exists to some extent) between the official end point of the GCSE syllabus and the official starting point of the 'A' level syllabus in modern foreign languages.

'A' level teachers were beginning to become aware of this phenomenon in 1988 with the first post-GCSE intake, and to cope with its implications. We grasped the nettle more tightly in 1989 and 1990. Staff in straight-through schools will probably have had more continuity of overview. Whereas at the college in question, there was a transfer both of institution and of teacher at 16+, the extent and implications of the sea change were not so easily appreciated except in the abstract. This was notwithstanding the 'cascade' in-service training given for the GCSE examination, teachers' panels, and liaison meetings between secondary schools and secondary colleges. Initially, little or no emphasis was placed on training 'A' level staff to bridge the gap between examination syllabuses, perhaps because it was not realised how big the transition now was.

Also, at that time, 'A' level coursebooks and other teaching resources mostly still assumed they were following on from the 'O' level end point and from its less communicative methodology. To visualise the gulf, one only has to think of the vast quantities of grammar-based 'O' level revision materials jettisoned virtually overnight when GCSE was implemented.

How will the new instructions concerning reading be reflected in the GCSE test papers?

- Will the concept of a defined vocabulary still be in force then? Should it be?
- What scope will be allowed for idiom and image if imaginative writing is rehabilitated and transactional activities are reduced?

Furthermore, will it be easier to weather the transition to 'A' level at 16+ if the increased emphasis on knowledge of language (language awareness), understanding of structure and reading strategies is put into practice in the secondary classroom as well as in National Curriculum policy documents?

Crystal ball gazing aside, it looks as if GCSE MFL (or their ultimate replacement in 1997) should dovetail more smoothly with more advanced language courses such as 'A' level than it does at present with respect to reading, to the educational advantage of all concerned.

'A' levels have latterly been redesigned to an extent, but let us hope that, if radical revisions of 'A' level courses occur, educational planners on both sides of the curriculum divide will co-ordinate their efforts, so that this divide is less of a gulf.

As yet there is no compulsory continuation of a foreign language beyond 16+ in England and Wales. Students can vote with their feet in their choice of 'A' levels or other post-16 courses. There is a well reported tendency to see a foreign language as more difficult than other syllabus options. It is scarcely surprising if some of the students questioned in this survey experienced the transition from GCSE to 'A' level French as harder than with English, since they were comparing reading fluency in a first language with that in a second language. This does bring home, though, the need for a structured progression in the reading difficulty of foreign language materials and the importance of other study aids and strategies to smooth the path of the foreign language reader.

Given the current diversification in post-16 foreign language take-up other than 'A' level, via NVQs, FLAW, BTEC, RSA and Institute of Linguists examinations, and given the numbers of students now engaged in post-18 continuation courses or taking up their foreign language again (after a two-year gap or longer since GCSE) as ancillary skills on BTEC HND and as adjuncts to business studies, European studies, law, politics and other non-foreign language degree courses, the present trend towards more self-study means that the foundations for student competence and autonomy as readers at GCSE need to be very firm. It is to be hoped that the new directions programmed into National Curriculum policy will result in this greater reader autonomy.

References

Aplin R, A Miller and H Starkey, *Orientations,* Pupil's book (Hodder and Stoughton, 1985)

Barnes D, *Actuellement* (Stanley Thornes, 1990)

Beeching K and B Page, *Contrastes* (Cambridge University Press, 1988)

Bell J, *Doing your research project: a guide for first-time researchers in education and social science* (Open University Press, 1987)

Brockman P and G Guarisco, *Horizons* (Thomas Nelson and Sons, 1987)

Corless F, H Corless and R Gaskell, *Signes du temps: vécu,* second edition (Hodder and Stoughton, 1991)

Etcherelli C, *Elise ou la vraie vie* (Denoel, 1967). The critical edition used here is by Roach J (Methuen, 1985)

Grellet F, *Developing reading skills* (Cambridge University Press, 1981)

Hogben L, *The mother tongue* (Secker and Warburg, 1964)

Humberstone P, *Débouchés* (Hodder and Stoughton, 1988)

Marland M (ed), *Language across the curriculum* (Heinemann, 1977)

Marks W T (ed), *Le témoignage de l'enfant de choeur* by Georges Simenon (Harrap, 1949)

McEwen S, G Pickard and M Smith, *Décollage* (Stanley Thornes, 1989)

Mort D, T Slack and R Hares, *Tout droit!* (John Murray, 1993)

Modern foreign languages non-statutory guidance (National Curriculum Council, 1992)

National Curriculum initial advice (The modern foreign languages working group, Department of Education and Science, 1990)

Nott D O (ed), *325000 francs* by Roger Vailland (The English Universities Press, 1955)

Nuttall, *Teaching reading skills in a foreign language* (Heinemann Educational, 1982)

Rowlinson, *Nous les Français* (Oxford University Press, 1987–)

Smith F, *Understanding reading — a psycholinguistic analysis of reading and learning to read* (New York: Holt, Rinehart and Winston, 1982)

Swarbrick A, *Reading for pleasure in a foreign language* (CILT, 1990)

Thorogood J and L King, *Bridging the gap: GCSE to 'A' level* (CILT, 1991)

Chapter 3
Reading literary texts at 'A' level: three case studies

by Liliane White

Although much has been written about the teaching of reading and literature in a foreign language, and various useful suggestions have been made, there is little practical guidance relating to 'A' level teaching and little hard evidence of how sixteen- to nineteen-year-olds cope with a literary component.

It was precisely in order to try to fill that gap that I decided to get involved in this piece of research and carry out the following case-studies. Below are extracts from an MPhil dissertation for submission at Southampton University.

History of the case studies

The case studies took place over the two years of the duration of the 'A' level course, from September 1989 till June 1991. During that time, four groups of students and their teachers, from three sixth form colleges in Hampshire collaborated with me.

Prior to the research, I had sent out a questionnaire to all sixth form colleges and institutions with a sixth form in the county, aiming at establishing who would be interested in taking part in the case-studies. I also gave a brief outline of what participation would involve. Many colleges were interested but only a few teachers seemed really keen to participate.

Finally three colleges were selected, one of them being my own establishment. The other two were chosen primarily because of the amount of interest expressed by particular teachers working there, but also because of the nature of the syllabus they used and for practical reasons such as distance and compatible timetables.

PARTICIPATING COLLEGES

The three colleges are referred to in this study as College 1, College 2 and College 3, and are all of comparable size, attracting between 1200 and 1500 students. They are within a fifteen mile radius of each other, but whereas Colleges 2 and 3 draw students mostly from an upper-middle class background, with a fair number coming from the independent sector, College 1 receives students from a mixture of social backgrounds and only a few from the independent sector.

In College 1, two groups were chosen: mine and that of the Head of Department who had expressed an interest in the case studies. Both groups were following the revised version of the Oxford syllabus which was to be offered in the college for the first time and would be examined by the Oxford Delegacy Of Local Examinations in 1991, one year after examination first began.

In Colleges 2 and 3, one group was selected in each college. There, students were being entered for the SUJB B examination offered by the Southern Universities' Joint Board, which had been used in the college for several years.

The four groups were of comparable size at the start with fourteen and fifteen students in each group in College 1, sixteen in College 2 and eighteen in College 3. In Colleges 2 and 3 the drop-out rate was quite considerable during the first year and as a consequence groups were merged and additional students joined the original reduced groups. In College 2, overall 'A' level teaching in French was shared between three teachers on a termly basis in the first year which meant that each teacher could specialise in one work of literature and study it with each of the groups in turn. In College 3, teaching was also shared between two teachers. Consequently, although at first only one teacher in each college expressed a real interest, in fact seven became involved because of the job share.

PLANS FOR DATA-GATHERING

I tried to divide attention as equally as possible between teachers and students and to focus not only on how students read, study and react to French literature, but also on how teachers approach it and what they feel about teaching it.

In concertation with the three teachers who had originally displayed an interest in the case studies, I decided:

* to observe the groups twice a term at mutually convenient dates;
* to interview the three main participants at the beginning of term 4 half-way through the course; and
* to ask students to fill in questionnaires at specific times.

Altogether three questionnaires and one cloze test were completed by the students of the four groups.

Aims of the case studies

The aim of the case studies was to follow a few groups of students and their teachers over the duration of their 'A' level course, in order to clarify a few issues relating to the study of French literature and the practice of extensive reading at sixth form level. It was hoped that valuable information could be obtained through class observation, questionnaires and teachers' interviews on the following points:

• Are post GCSE students well prepared to embark on a programme of extensive reading in French and study of literary texts?
• Is some form of literature study desirable and realistic at sixth form level ?
• To what extent is the study of literature in the foreign language beneficial to the students in terms of linguistic and personal development?
• What approaches to extensive reading and literature study seem to work well in an 'A' level class?

I shall tackle the teachers' interviews first.

THE TEACHERS' INTERVIEWS

In Colleges 1 and 2, the interviewees were also the Heads of Department and therefore responsible for the reading/literature policy of their college. In College 3, the teacher interviewed had previously written an MEd on the role and nature of extensive reading and was committed to a reading programme. To preserve the teachers' anonymity, I shall refer to them in this study with the initials A, B, C. Teacher A was teaching in College 3, Teacher B in College 2 and Teacher C in College 1.

Syllabuses

First of all, each teacher was asked to establish which syllabus they were using: both Teachers A and B were following the SUJB B syllabus which was at the time the most widely used in Hampshire and the only one to accredit extensive reading in the examination, whereas Teacher C had just changed to the revised Oxford syllabus after years of using SUJB B. Teacher A, however, announced that they too, would in a year's time be changing to the revised Oxford syllabus because they felt that SUJB B was somehow obsolete and did not make enough use of the target language.

PERCEIVED STRENGTHS AND WEAKNESSES OF THE SYLLABUSES

I shall concentrate here on reporting what they thought of as the strengths and weaknesses of the syllabuses in relation to reading and the way in which it was being examined.

Assessing how extensive reading was examined in the oral exam, Teacher A described as 'ridiculous' the five minutes allocated to the discussion of two years' reading. Teachers B and C agreed with her while Teacher A also stressed that having worked as an oral examiner, she had discovered 'an enormous discrepancy' between the amount of literature preparation that had been done in the various establishments (a few books compared to a dozen). She summed up her feelings by saying that:

> 'the syllabus can allow for the promotion and encouragement of reading but the trouble is that it is fairly open and it is left to the teacher, the department and the students to actually decide what emphasis they are going to give it.'

On a positive note, Teacher B emphasised that:

> 'SUJB B is the only syllabus which actually provides a stick/ carrot to encourage students to read as widely as possible.'

and she concluded:

> 'It is one of the major reasons why we are stuck with the syllabus, because there are so many effects from reading as far as improvement of language is concerned other than just the reading skills, the knock-on effect.'

Personally, although I did not record my views, my feelings were closer to that teacher's and I feared that moving away from a syllabus which makes extensive reading an element of the examination (even if somewhat inadequately), could have serious repercussions on the amount our students read.

Teacher A did not share this worry and instead felt that the revised Oxford syllabus could allow the students more contact with literature and more involvement, and she added:

> 'We think that the link between literature and other topics is quite valuable.'

As I am finalising my research, SUJB B is no longer in existence and two out of these three colleges have been using the revised Oxford syllabus. The remaining college opted instead for a new modular syllabus.

GCSE to 'A' level

THE INFAMOUS GAP

The next issue tackled in the interviews was that of the infamous 'gap' between GCSE and 'A' level and the standard of reading proficiency attained through GCSE.

Teacher C was finding that reading is a much greater difficulty post-GCSE than it was after 'O' level. She thought that this was due to some extent to the nature of current GCSE syllabuses and the way they test reading. She stressed that there was a heavy emphasis on transactional language and current affairs. Teacher B supported her by adding:

> 'It tends to be so functional . . . they will have done very little work on figurative expressions.'

Teacher C emphasised too, that the very nature of the reading comprehension tests which focus on 'picking up details here and there', and favour factual understanding to the detriment of overall comprehension, restricts the reader and is not conducive to the development of effective reading skills.

For all these reasons, and the fact that in-coming students are only used to reading fairly short articles, Teacher A has had to defer the introduction of literary texts till much later on in the year than she used to. She says:

> 'We've found that students coming in with GCSE had done so little reading that to plunge them straight into even a play was asking too much of them.'

Consequently if we are to believe these teachers and generalise somewhat, it appears that post-GCSE students are ill prepared for an exploration into the world of fiction which makes much use of figurative and imaginative vocabulary and requires that students process large amounts of text efficiently.

Aims for reading

In the third part of the interview, teachers were asked to explain why they thought that extensive reading/literature was a valuable exercise and to specify what their aims were.

Teacher B insisted that her aims were very broad:

* to get them reading for their own good and their own pleasure;
* to give them some love of reading in a foreign language.

Teacher A, too, talked of:

* intellectual satisfaction, inspiring students with works selected for them.

For these teachers, instilling into their students some of the enthusiasm that they themselves feel for reading seems to be a driving force. Teacher B stressed too that students should:

* develop confidence in their own reading ability.

> 'By the end of the second year, I would aim to have a fairly fluent reader and for the students to have acquired strategies even if we haven't directly given them, by which they can pick up a paperback in France, go to a library in France and sit down and read.'

Interestingly, in these days when 'differentiation' along with 'transition' appear to be key-words for FL teaching, Teacher A mentioned that:

> 'reading in the foreign language is a very worthwhile exercise because it allows us to differentiate between our students in catering to their individual needs, their individual responsiveness in literature.'

All three teachers agreed, too, that one of the major benefits derived from reading extensively is that:

* it improves the students' linguistic skills.

Teacher C stressed that:

> 'We get the students to absorb in the passive sense, a massive amount of language which there would be no chance whatsoever of getting across in class or through very specifically directed tasks.'

Teacher B talked of:

> '. . . the acquisition of vocabulary in a fairly painless way, the feel for the language . . . which will improve some of the written and probably spoken language to a certain degree.'

AIMS CHANGE FROM YEAR 1 TO YEAR 2

Teacher C mentioned that her aims change from year 1 to year 2:

> 'In year 1, the focus is very much on using the ideas in order to use the language and to get them to recycle quite a lot of what they have read.'

In year 2, however, there is for Teacher C a definite shift from language work to the study of ideas and issues which will personally involve the students. She says:

> *'In the second year, we are very, very much more looking at the ideas and, I would like to be able to say, at the way in which the author had constructed the novel/play.'*

However, Teacher C stressed that experience has shown her that at 'A' level, only *'one or two students in each group are going to be capable of sustaining that kind of discussion'*. This is why instead of focusing on a formal critical appreciation of the book, she prefers to conduct discussion at a lower level and involve all the students personally.

She added:

> *'I do feel that at this stage in their lives, the sixteen to nineteen stage, students are confronted with very confusing decisions, discoveries about themselves, discoveries about other people and I think that the great value of literature for them is the ability to see that other people get in the same jams that they do, perhaps in a more dramatic way , to be able to identify with these people, to be able to work out some of their own conflicts.'*

Teacher C then gave the example of some students who, after discussing in class *L'étranger* and the issue of the treatment of old people, completely reviewed their position. One member of the group had exposed the personal dilemma confronting his family and the whole group had discussed the issue in a mature and sensitive way.

Teacher C believes, too, that in our televised age, books still provide the best means of achieving this personal development in a vicarious way:

> *'Films and television series allow for this but only in a fairly superficial kind of way because it is all presented for you on a plate.They come to terms with things in their own life much more through reading and thinking about it and discussing it in a novel.'*

And she adds:

> *'That is the real reason why I believe in the study of literature.'*

In such a context literary works are no longer in themselves the end of the study, but instead as Teacher B put it:

> *'The book becomes a springboard, an excuse to talk about whatever topic may come out of the book.'*

These three teachers seemed very much in agreement on what they aim to achieve: although all stressed the importance of reading to improve language skills, they put the emphasis on the emotional and intellectual benefits which the students can derive from such exposure.

Extensive reading or study of literature?

Very closely related to this is the issue of the nature of the exercise undertaken in the sixth form by the students and their teachers.

When asked whether she thought that what they did was extensive reading or already an introduction to literary appreciation, Teacher B answered very clearly:

> *'I would like to think that it was reading, certainly as far as their personal reading is concerned and even in class, we are not looking really in great detail at analysis of character . . . it is an excuse for discussion really much more than literature, although very occasionally we look at style with* L'étranger *for instance, because that is intrinsically linked with the book itself but normally no.'*

Teacher C for her part saw the exercise more as an aspect of the personal development of the students rather than as a way of developing their ability to appreciate literature in the critical sense. She explained this by the fact that *'many are not used to reading literature, novels, plays in any language whatsoever'*, and that consequently *'very few have any kind of literary appreciation at all'*. Thirdly, the additional barrier of a foreign language renders the task almost impossible except for a very few.

Teacher A's answer was more complex as she believes that some students are more receptive than others, and can take reading one step further. She said:

> *'It depends on how receptive the individual student is, it is not a question of whether they have the literary equipment, the literary critic equipment through having done English 'A' level concurrently with French, it is more a question of whether they are individually receptive to literature and that's going to demand a certain level of comprehension.'*

She qualified this last remark by adding:

> *'It is partly linguistic, it is also cultural awareness as they come to a novel with the ability to pick up the clues they are given and perhaps respond to them.'*

PERSONAL INTERACTION WITH THE TEXT

It seems that for Teacher C and the other two as well, personal interaction with the text is the key to some form of literary appreciation rather than the ability to discuss the literary merits of a book. Although all three were reluctant to refer to their reading activities as study or teaching of literature, they all conceded that the guided reading carried out in class and backed up by home and class activities, probably represents a small step towards an appreciation of literature.

Teacher C said:

> 'We ask them to stand back and to think about the literature imaginatively, I think that is coming close to bridging a gap between their own experience of literature and real literary appreciation.'

The teacher's role

FACILITATION — ANIMATION

How do these teachers perceive their own role? All three, using the current jargon, saw themselves first of all, in their own words, as facilitators. Pointing out, for instance, that students need help when selecting books for personal reading, Teacher C mentioned that it is her responsibility to:

> 'make sure that they don't read anything that is going to be completely beyond their linguistic competence or their conceptual ability or, in fact, their kind of philosophical understanding of life.'

She also believes in being:

> 'a sounding board for what they have understood of the plot first of all, because there is no doubt about it, not all of them do understand the plot.'

She will intervene and correct their ideas if comprehension is impaired but once basic understanding has been attained by all, she likes to step back and become a kind of 'chair for discussion'. She explains that:

> 'the ideal lesson would be one in which (she) literally did virtually nothing but moved from group to group listening to what they said, helping them when they have disagreements among themselves and . . . trying to pop in the odd question here and there to get them to go a little further along their line of thinking.'

She admits, however, that at 'A' level, this is more wishful thinking than reality:

> 'I have to be honest and say that that does not happen a great
> deal, it does not happen at all in the first year at the moment
> because I am finding that reading is a much greater difficulty
> post-GCSE than it was post-'O' level . . . but in the second year
> really it can get to that stage with a good group.'

In a similar way, Teacher A talked of being *une animatrice,* a manager getting them talking about their reading. Certainly none of them believed that teachers should hold centre-stage and be telling students what to think. Teacher C admitted that very often she has to resist pressure from the students who want to know what her opinions are. If she does volunteer an opinion, they all say: 'Ah! That must be the right answer'. She added:

> 'I don't want them ever to think that there is a right answer to
> anything because I don't. The text happens, I mean the work of
> literature happens in between the page and the reader and it's
> up to them really what they make of it, once they have actually
> understood the language.'

Although Teachers A and B did not elaborate as much on that aspect of their role as Teacher C, I very much felt that they thought along similar lines. They, for their part, insisted on the seemingly contradictory need in view of what has just been said, for the teacher to be 'a disciplinarian'.

INTELLECTUAL DISCIPLINE

Teacher B emphasised that it was necessary to be tough with students and to set them strict deadlines for finishing books, that there must be some 'structured reading time', in order to give reading a high status and a high priority. Similarly, Teacher A said that students must be made to read and frequently reminded of the value of the exercise. Confronted with the need to give extensive reading a high status in a syllabus which encourages it but does not reward it adequately, one can see why the two teachers still using SUJB B, felt the need for discipline and structure. Interestingly, Teacher C working from the Oxford syllabus, where literature represents one topic among others, did not highlight the same need.

Personal response and the traditional literary approach

It has already become evident that all three teachers actively encourage their students to experience and respond personally to the books they read in class on their own. Consequently, their feelings on the traditional approach which was heavily teacher centred and relied on literary criticism and ready-made judgments will come as no surprise.

REJECTION OF TRADITIONAL APPROACH

Teacher B expressed her rejection of the former method most clearly and has evolved her teaching method in reaction to it:

> *'I am thinking back to my old days at 'A' level. It is almost as if you know that the teacher is wanting certain listed responses, and the examiner by extension, so trying to get away from that and really encouraging the students to be personal and not to make them feel that they are reacting correctly or incorrectly.'*

Thinking back she was very critical of the way she was taught:

> *'We did four set books and that's all we read in the course of two years, . . . we did line by line translation into English and discussion in English of the characters and the vocabulary. The teacher would give us notes on the characters and what have you, . . . and we were required to write a three hour paper . . . I think it can be absolutely deadly. Even if you are interested in literature it is such an unimaginative approach and of course not doing an awful lot of good for your language skills.'*

Teacher C, seems to have found in the revised Oxford syllabus the very antidote to this impersonal and personalised approach. She said:

> *'The Oxford Examination Board makes it absolutely clear that they don't want students to go away and read accounts by critics, because they want nothing to interfere with that personal critical response and some of the questions they set are in fact quite individualistic and some would even think bizarre.'*

FURTHER EXPLOITATION OF TEXTS

She explained that in the written exam those who have chosen the literary option might for instance be encouraged to take various scenes from the novel and turn them into a film script, and demonstrate their understanding of the novel from that point of view. Her opinion of the task was that *'it is quite interesting, quite challenging but a very valid exercise in fact in the literary sense.'*

Closely related to that comment is that of Teacher A who believes that books can be used as stimuli for the creativity of the students and said: *'The work we do, based on that reading, will encourage response, creative writing for example.'*

Methodology

I had been surprised to find out that the three teachers held very similar views on most points. This could be explained by the fact they were very much in the same age group (late 30s to mid 40s), but more likely by the fact that all three had been recently actively involved in research on reading and literary teaching, either personally (Teachers A and B) or indirectly (Teacher C).

DIFFERENCES IN METHODS

Small differences appeared, however, when we discussed methodology. The most striking one I found concerned the time when each college chooses to introduce their students to their first unsimplified book. In College 2, they believe that it can be done immediately in September, whereas in Colleges 1 and 3 teachers prefer to wait until the beginning of the second term.

In those two colleges, according to Teachers C and A, students are gradually introduced to extensive reading once some basic reading skills have been established and students have read a few easy short stories like *Le petit Nicolas* by Sempé and one simplified reading book of the *Easy Reader* type. Teacher A in College 1 believes in devoting five or six sessions to developing reading skills such as:

- strategies for comprehension;
- strategies for avoiding getting bogged down;
- instilling regular reading habits;
- giving the students pride in their achievement.

Teacher C for her part admits to using no more than a session because of lack of time though she wishes she did more and believes that a whole series of worksheets are required for teaching those specific skills as well as a departmental policy.

In College 2 however, this intermediate stage takes place during the Summer holidays preceding the beginning of the course. During Induction Day in July, potential students collect reading material to be studied over the holidays and answer comprehension questions on the text in English thus saving valuable time according to Teacher B.

SIMILARITIES IN METHODS

Apart from this rather striking difference, the three teachers interviewed seem to use very similar teaching methods.

All three teachers say that they operate a reading programme including both independent and class activities. The class activities according to them allow for both group work and whole class discussion with the support of reading-guides in French on which the students work at home prior to the lesson. The three teachers all declared themselves committed to using the target language in the reading/literature lesson and they encourage their students to recycle the language from the texts as much as possible mostly through oral work but occasionally in writing.

Conclusion to the teachers' interviews

Apart from a few marginal differences, all three teachers seem committed to the study of literary texts and seem to share the same outlook as well as very similar teaching methods. They put the emphasis before all on a direct personal response to the texts uninfluenced by the writing of critics and for that reason often select books that are not recognised as classics but to which students can relate.

CLASSROOM PRACTICE

From September 1989 till June 1991 when examinations started, I was in close contact with the French departments of the three colleges taking part in the case studies and sat through lessons at least once a term, observing and taking notes. Occasionally teachers would draw me into discussions and at specific times of the course I distributed questionnaires for students to fill in at home.

Three groups are under scrutiny (my own group is excluded here, as I found it impossible to observe my own teaching objectively). They are: Group 1 for College 1, Group 2 for College 2 and Group 3 for College 3.

Thematic analysis of the observational data

After a preliminary review of the data collected over 18 months, it seemed to me that it could be grouped for analysis under four themes:

- The first set of data would include information on the types of books studied by the target groups at 'A' level.
- A second set of data would relate to the nature of the activities taking place in the lessons and would establish the relative emphasis placed on the texts or on language development. It would also address the contentious issue of systematic use of the target language.

- The third group of data would allow us to determine whether there was some evidence of literary appreciation among the students.
- The fourth group would contain data relating to the students' involvement and the nature of their response as well as information concerning the nature of the role played by the teachers.

Data relating to the selection of texts

Let us review first of all the information relating to the types of books being selected for class study by the three colleges.

The list runs as follows and is in chronological order:

TERM 1	
Lettres de mon moulin (simplified edition) (Daudet)	College 1
Le petit prince (Saint-Exupéry)	College 2
Tintin and other cartoons (Hergé)	College 3
TERM 2	
Les jeux sont faits (Sartre) and *Paroles* (Prévert)	College 1
L'étranger (Camus)	College 2
Le petit prince (Saint-Exupéry)	College 3
TERM 3	
L'étranger (Camus)	College 1
Les mains sales (Sartre)	College 2
Antigone (Anouilh)	College 3
TERM 4	
L'étranger (Camus)	
and *Les petits enfants du siècle* (Rochefort)	College 1
Les petits enfants du siècle (Rochefort)	College 2
Les mains sales (Sartre)	College 3
TERM 5	
None	College 1
Elise ou la vraie vie (Etcherelli)	College 2
None	College 3

The books were twentieth century works (apart from Daudet's), well-known and generally recognised as modern classics with the exception of Hergé's cartoons, *Les petits enfants du siècle* and *Elise ou la vraie vie* which were written in the 1950s and have not yet reached the status of classics.

Although there are slight variations between colleges, e.g. *L'étranger* studied during term 2 in College 2 and terms 3/4 in College 1, one is still struck by how similar the choices were although neither of the two syllabuses in use specified certain titles. Nobody for instance elected to study *Le petit prince* in term 5 or *Elise ou la vraie vie* in term 1. To ask oneself: why not? is also to address the issue of what makes a book easy or difficult. I shall try to answer that question later on.

Most of the students seemed to be coping quite well with the books, getting involved in discussions, some more than others as is usual, and appearing to derive pleasure from their reading. However, when observing, I could not help noticing that in Colleges 2 and 3, the two groups studying *Les mains sales* were really struggling through the political aspects of the play and showed very little understanding of the plot. For each group, the tutor had to interrupt the discussion and provide additional explanations on the political set-up.

For *Elise ou la vraie vie,* problems seemed to arise from the length of the novel as well as the technical nature of the vocabulary used to describe working conditions in a car factory. When asked by Teacher F to evaluate the advantages and disadvantages of studying the book at 'A' level, several students from Group 2 mentioned vocabulary and length as major disadvantages while a few also complained about the slow pace of the narrative and the lack of action in the first part of the book.

Variations

SYSTEMATIC CONSULTATION OF STUDENTS

It appeared to me that College 2 was the only one to conduct systematic consultations of students as soon as the book had been finished. I was there when they took place both for *Le petit prince* and *Elise ou la vraie vie* and found the feedback very enlightening because it provided first-hand information on what makes a book difficult for students as well as enjoyable. The Head of Department said that it was departmental policy to ask for the students' opinion because they learnt quite a lot from their responses, although they had occasionally encountered conflicting opinions between groups.

DIFFERING REACTIONS

Some interesting variations, too, occurred when the same book was being studied by different groups and under different teachers. When asked by Teacher B to comment on *Le petit prince,* the response from Group 2 was overwhelming. I shall quote from my notes here:

'Out of fifteen students, eleven found it excellent, three had mixed feelings and one had disliked it but admitted not having spent much time on it. Teacher B was amazed by the results, said that it was the first time she had encountered such a positive response and declared herself delighted with the findings.'

I found no evidence of such enthusiasm in College 3. There, students' opinion was much more divided, with about one third admitting to me when I asked them individually that they had not been able to go beyond the storyline. For them it was just a rather weird children's story.

EFFECTS OF TEACHER ENTHUSIASM

I could not help concluding that the students' reaction must undoubtedly be linked with the level of enthusiasm generated by the teacher, even accepting that some groups are more receptive than others. In her interview Teacher B admitted that *Le petit prince* is one of her favourite books, her *pièce de résistance* and that she greatly enjoys teaching it. I did not in the course of my observations encounter again such contagious interest for a book.

Progression

As mentioned earlier, there seemed to be a consensus among the teachers that some books are more suitable than others at a certain time of the course and looking at the list of texts being studied, it seemed as if linguistic criteria must have been the decisive factors when operating the selection.

ACCESSIBILITY TO STUDENTS

It is usually recognised that the carefully selected language (structures and vocabulary) of a simplified reader such as *Lettres de mon moulin* is more accessible to students at the beginning of an 'A' level course than unabridged versions. Similarly, the structures and vocabulary used by Saint-Exupéry in a book primarily intended for children can be understood without too much trouble in the early parts of the sixth form. The language of *Paroles* and *Les jeux sont faits* did not seem to present the students with a problem either although both were studied early on in the course. In the case of *L'étranger*, the vocabulary is mostly known and the use of the perfect tense for the narrative instead of the customary but less well-known past historic, makes comprehension less of a hurdle for first year students. Teachers admitted that they left *Elise ou la vraie vie* and *Les petits enfants du siècle* till the second year because of the technical vocabulary used in the former one and the considerable amount of slang and colloquialisms in the latter.

PREPARATORY SHEETS

In College 1, it was felt that students were treading on such unfamiliar ground with *Les petits enfants du siècle* that they were given preparatory work on the language of the book. They all received three sheets of slang and colloquial expressions recurring in the novel and had to provide equivalents for them in standard French. That initiative proved very useful later on and eased somewhat the language problem.

PRIOR KNOWLEDGE

However, selecting a book solely from the point of view of accessibility of the language can lead to students having a rather unhappy experience of the book. That was well illustrated by students' reaction to *Les mains sales*.

The play was studied in term 3 in College 2 and term 4 in College 3, and on both occasions students were struggling to make sense of the plot. The difficulty did not arise from the language of the play which is indeed quite accessible but from the political set-up and the level of political awareness which it requires and which seventeen- to eighteen-year-olds rarely possess. In spite of the guidance provided by signpost questions, teachers were several times called upon to feed complementary information or to correct misinterpretation.

The same occurred to a lesser degree in the group I observed with *Antigone* as students had little or no prior knowledge of the society and mythology of Ancient Greece. These two examples point to the need to take into account the accessibility of the background, whether it is political, historical or cultural.

SEEING BEYOND THE STORY-LINE

A slightly different situation arose with *L'étranger*. Although the language is simple and the background knowledge required more familiar, the students I observed often found it difficult to rise to the level of intellectual and philosophical sophistication required to tackle the issues arising from the novel. Although most coped well with the issue of the death penalty, only a few could address in any depth the key issues of alienation from society, hypocrisy of the justice system and religion. Many answers given in class revealed that they could not really see beyond the story line. (The same of course was also true in the case of *Le petit prince* and also *Antigone* where few could see the possible link with terrorism.)

As a consequence of the real difficulties experienced by the students on an intellectual level, in College 1 the study of *L'étranger* has now been postponed to year 2, by which time it is hoped that students will have matured both intellectually and emotionally.

WHAT MAKES A BOOK EASY OR DIFFICULT?

To answer the question which I asked earlier about what makes a book easy or difficult, one could say after studying the data that it is very much a combination of language, background knowledge, intellectual and emotional depth as well as length. (*Elise ou la vraie vie* is a long book.)

Nevertheless, if we are to hold our students' interest and make the study of literary text a rewarding experience then some way has to be found to include criteria other than purely linguistic.

Evaluation

It appears therefore that the issue of suitability of texts and progression was mostly viewed in language terms in the three colleges, and that criteria relating to cultural and historical background knowledge as well as intellectual and emotional maturity were not sufficiently taken on board at the time. One could argue of course that some of these criteria are quite subjective, that different groups have different requirements and that it is very difficult to conciliate all the criteria within the limits of availability and a tight budget.

When one comes to evaluate the choices made by the teachers, there is no doubt that the result is largely positive. On the whole it worked well as shown by the involvement and enjoyment expressed by the majority of students.

I felt that critics like Chambers, Corless, Reeves, Benton and Brumfit, to quote but a few, would have been satisfied with such texts. All of them insist on the need to select:

> '*modern texts which offer the sixth form student insights into human issues which he can immediately relate to and talk about.*' (Corless, 1977: 167)

There is no doubt to me either that consulting students is an excellent way of judging the validity of a book: in College 2, I noticed that it seemed to be regular practice and it is quite likely that Teacher F may review her choice of *Elise ou la vraie vie* in the light of her students' criticisms.

I nevertheless felt that some of these teachers could have heeded Corless's words of caution that:

> '*the texts should more particularly be chosen with due regard for the linguistic and maturational levels of the sixth former and should not be so long as to appear like some literary Everest towering before him.*' (Corless, 1977: 167)

Out of all these books, only *Elise ou la vraie vie* and probably *Les mains sales* might not have fitted the criteria.

Language learning activities in the literature class and use of the target language

Let us now review the data relating to the type of activities I encountered in the lessons, to establish whether the emphasis was placed on language learning or some form of literary appreciation. I shall also examine what use was made of the target language and the advantages and possible disadvantages of such practice.

GENERAL FEATURES OF PRACTICE

In all three colleges there was certainly plenty of evidence of language at work in the lessons, although the literature/reading lesson was clearly separate from the other purely language sessions. In all cases between 55 and 60 minutes per week were allocated to the reading and study of literary texts, except for the first half term in Colleges 1 and 3 when they were gently phased in. Right from the start of the course for College 2 and from the second half term for Colleges 1 and 3, students were required to read substantial amounts of simplified (College 1) or authentic literary French. Students were exposed to much greater quantities of French than they had been used to for GCSE and of a different register with little in common with the functional register in use at GCSE level. Not only were they required to read from the book but also to answer questions, be ready to discuss in class, take part in role plays and eventually write a summary or essay on the text all in the target language. This seemed common practice in all three colleges but because of lack of space in this study, I shall mainly dip into the data collected in College 2, where the same group of students was taught by four teachers over eighteen months and where I witnessed a variety of teaching styles.

Term 1 in College 2: Teacher B

The first literature class I observed in College 2 was taken by Teacher B and dealt with *Le petit prince*. Prior to my visit, the group had prepared answers to questions in French from Chapter 23 onwards, for homework. This chapter features a merchant selling magic pills which replace food and drink and therefore save time. Students were given a few minutes to compare notes and discuss their answers with each other in the target language. Then, Teacher B led the class into a discussion based on the work done at home and focusing on the students' personal attitude towards food and drink. The answers which had been prepared came readily. I quote here from my notes:

> 'Students were asked to say whether they enjoy eating and
> drinking, what is their favourite food and drink. The group was
> responding well and Teacher B extended the questions to how

long they or their parents spend shopping and cooking each week and how much time they could save by taking the pills. Finally they were asked whether they would be in favour of using them and all except one were against it and alleging that they needed an excuse to go to the pub.'

USE OF TARGET LANGUAGE

The level of participation and enthusiasm was high, possibly because of the familiarity of the vocabulary amply covered at GCSE, but also I thought because the students felt personally involved. The target language was used throughout this activity and for the rest of the lesson which focused partly on comprehension of the remainder of the plot, partly on the students' evaluation of the book and partly on the correction of a crossword and quiz all borrowed from the *Folio Junior* edition.

'AN EXCUSE FOR DISCUSSION'

I felt that this particular lesson was very much a language lesson not only because of the amount of target language used but also because language practice was very much the teacher's prime concern. The book came second and merely provided 'an excuse for discussion' as Teacher B stated later on in her interview.

Term 2 in College 2: Teacher D

In the same college, in term 2, I witnessed some evidence of language work even more loosely related to the text. The students by then were being taught by Teacher D and were studying *L'étranger* Chapter 3, Part 2. The teacher (who had little prior experience of studying literary texts with students) had decided to use the support pack on the book produced by the Oxford Delegacy.

LANGUAGE EXERCISE GAME

The first twenty minutes of the lesson were taken up by a language exercise on verbs borrowed from the pack. The teacher had decided to turn it into a game: the class was divided into two teams, each student being given a number and competing with a member of the other team to be the first to give the correct answer. Initially, the students responded with enthusiasm, which started to wane after the first ten minutes and prompted Teacher D to abandon the activity soon after. The only link of the activity to the book was that the verbs had been lifted from the text and it was purely a grammatical exercise.

TEACHER'S INTERVENTIONS

After the lesson, Teacher D voiced her reservations regarding the pack saying that she thought it contained too many language exercises and wondering whether the Oxford Delegacy had in mind that literary texts should be studied mostly to aid language development. The remaining 35 minutes of the session were spent on activities devised by her and testing comprehension of the chapter which features the trial of Meursault, a white man accused of killing an Arab. Group work followed by class discussion took place on the following issues: 'Est-il accusé d'avoir enterré sa mère ou d'avoir tué un homme?' and: 'Quelles sont vos impressions de la Justice et qu'est-ce que cela vous dit des idées de Camus?' Students found the questions hard and many remained silent, possibly because they could not express themselves adequately in the target language. The most fluent and able offered interesting and perceptive comments, however, revealing a good degree of understanding of the ideas of the novel and the ability to analyse and rise above the text.

REFLECTING ON IMPLICATIONS

Altogether this was a varied lesson with some language work almost unrelated to the text, followed by some exploratory pair work very much focused on the text. Students were asked to reflect on the implications of the characters' actions and abstract themselves from the plot in order to pass a value judgement on the judicial system, as well as try to access the writer's point of view through his account of the court case. For some of them this was a difficult exercise.

The target language was used throughout but I felt that students who had difficulty expressing their point of view in French should have been given the chance to express themselves in English, as it seemed a great pity that valuable responses had been wasted because of an over-insistence on the use of the target language.

Term 3 in College 2: Teacher E

The lesson I observed in term 3 under Teacher E was totally different from the previous two. The students were studying *Les mains sales* by Sartre and had reached Scene II of the *Quatrième Tableau*. Although a support pack similar to that for *L'étranger* does exist, Teacher E was not using it. The students had read Scenes II and III at home but this time without the support of questions.

RECAPPING THE PLOT

The lesson began with the teacher asking one volunteer to recap on the plot so far. When he asked for the names of the three political parties involved, it became apparent that the students were finding the question quite difficult. More questioning in the target language followed until comprehension of the scene had been established.

Some of the questions dealt with precise points and from time to time Teacher E would feed in complementary information when it was obvious that the students had misunderstood or missed an important point. Occasionally, he translated a line which was proving difficult. Students were then asked to volunteer to read the parts of the three characters. The teacher intervened frequently to correct pronunciation, explain key-words, ask further questions and again feed in supplementary information. He mentioned Jessica's inferiority complex and related it to existentialism. Faced with blank looks from the students, he then asked if any one knew what this meant and proceeded to explain when no one replied. Some asked further questions, some looked lost and started fidgetting and chatting quietly. Finally, Teacher E played an English version of the scene and students followed in their books. The same pattern was repeated for Scene III.

This lesson was different from the previous two as the emphasis was very much on content rather than on language work and although French was spoken most of the time, there was more use of English by the teacher and occasionally by the students who were not rebuked for doing so. I asked some students informally after the lesson, whether hearing the scenes in English had helped them and they all agreed that they now had a clearer idea of what was happening.

Terms 4 and 5 in College 2: Teacher F

During the second year, students in College 2 kept the same teacher and read *Les petits enfants du siècle* by Rochefort in term 4 and *Elise ou la vraie vie* by Etcherelli in term 5.

PREPARING AN IMAGINARY DIALOGUE

For the lesson I attended in term 4, they had prepared at home an imaginary dialogue between the main character Josyane and her Algerian friend Fatima. The characters had met while waiting to talk to the careers' adviser and were supposed to discuss their home life, families, feelings about school and their plans for the future. This was meant as a follow-up activity to Chapter 4. The teacher had instructed the group to make ample use of the colloquialisms and slang found in the novel.

When each pair of students presented their dialogue to the class, it was evident that:

• not only were most re-using vocabulary effectively; but also that

- their interpretation of the characters was consistent with their portrayal in the novel; and
- revealed a good understanding of Fatima and Josyane's home background.

As expected, some presentations were better than others, with the poorer ones remaining superficial and making use of only a limited range of vocabulary.

EXTRAPOLATION TO STUDENTS' PERSONAL PLANS

Teacher F only intervened when students were clearly not understood by the rest of the class. The whole exercise lasted about twenty minutes, after which the students were allocated another ten minutes to prepare a dialogue in which they would discuss their own plans for the following year, taking care to use the informal register found in the book. It appeared that some words and expressions were firm favourites: *bagnole* for car was one, *boulot*, *con*, *foutre* were others. Those words were being used enthusiastically though not always in the right context: '*Qu'est-ce que tu foutras l'an prochain?*' — '*Oh, je foutrai les maths et la physique à l'université de Southampton!*' As earlier on, some presentations were much better than others but on average twenty or so words and expressions had been mostly successfully recycled and made their own by the students.

In many ways this lesson was a good example of vocabulary and structures being actively recycled and there was evidence that most students had internalised some elements of French slang, a register until then mostly unknown to them.

USE OF TARGET LANGUAGE TO INTERACT WITH THE CHARACTERS

The target language was used constantly, but at the same time in the case of the first activity it was also a way of interacting with the characters, of identifying with them and accessing the meaning of the book in a personal way.

During term 5, I sat through three sessions based on *Elise ou la vraie vie*. One of the lessons I observed was very similar to the one previously described. The students had to imagine that Henri, the heroine's brother, was interviewing Elise and her Algerian lover Arezki. They were asked to identify with the characters and to focus on racial incidents that had occurred in the book. The exercise served the dual purpose of encouraging use of the target language but also of reinforcing understanding of the characters' feelings and place in society. The other two lessons were of a different nature and I shall review them when I deal with the issue of literary appreciation.

Evaluation

Let us try to establish what critics like Chambers, Carter, Corless and Widdowson, to quote but a few names, would have thought of these lessons. I believe that they would have approved of the way in which literary texts were being used to support linguistic development. Corless, for instance, would have found evidence that students were effectively recycling some of the language from the texts and 'eventually making it (his) their own'. However, although language and literature teaching activities were integrated, there was also evidence that the aim of most of the lessons was not purely linguistic. Most teachers appeared to believe that students should also respond to literature personally and experience it through activities encouraging identification with the characters. Benton and Brumfit would certainly have recognised some of the principles they advocate at work.

The class observations also threw an interesting light on the issue of the use of the target language and the current view backed by modern language advisers that all transactions should be carried out in the foreign language. I believe that modern languages teachers should not be made to feel guilty for using English when they see fit as they are the best judges of their groups' limitations. Just as it is my opinion that literature and language should go hand in hand and that we should certainly not go back to the old days when literature was entirely taught in English, I still think that there is some place for English in the reading/ literature lesson:

- It was obvious in certain lessons that students were becoming very frustrated for not being able to express their true feelings in the target language.

I believe that their personal response would have been much richer if only Teacher D had allowed them to revert to English for example. On the other hand, Teacher C and F who gave them that opportunity enhanced the quality of their experience.

I would not go as far as Neather (1975: 132–138) who once advocated the use of English translations to improve comprehension; I don't entirely agree either with Teacher E who played the English version of *Les mains sales,* although it was obvious that it helped comprehension. I would have preferred to keep to the target language here and if it was available play the French version of the play or read some extracts aloud to the group as I am convinced that intonation would have helped the students a great deal. I would however go along with Chambers who, like Teacher C and F, thinks that inflexible use of the target language can seriously damage the students' response. This is what he wrote:

> *'If a pupil feels strongly that he/she has something of value to contribute, he/she should be allowed to do so whatever the language. The exclusion of English could be positively damaging in terms of motivation and attitude.'* (Chambers, 1991: 6)

Some evidence of literary awareness

My point now is to try to establish through the information I gathered, whether there is evidence that some form of literary awareness was encouraged and developed during the lessons I observed. What I observed in College 2 during two lessons in term 5 seem to indicate that this was being attempted.

GENERAL FEATURES OF PRACTICE

During the first lesson, the students had reached the second half of *Elise ou la vraie vie,* with the section recounting Elise's first encounter of the conveyor belt in the car factory. After general understanding of the section had been established, Teacher F gave the class fifteen minutes to carry out the following task: *'Essayez d'identifier l'image dominante pour décrire la chaîne.'* Some students soon appeared to be finding the question difficult and the teacher had to go round to clarify the task to some and to explain problematic words to others. After a while, it became obvious that most had picked up the image of the snake, of the boa which swallows the workers. Once the concept of imagery had been established, Teacher B continued by asking the class to reflect on the use of images in the book and to select precise examples. Many students were struggling, some picking up comparisons rather than images, others just out of their depth. To help them, Teacher F read out extracts of a journalistic account by Robert Lindhardt, *L'établi*, and encouraged them to draw comparisons between the two writing styles. The students listened and one or two agreed that the texts were written quite differently, but on the whole there was very little response from the class nor did they seem terribly interested.

STYLE AND IMAGERY

I believe that this preoccupation with style and imagery goes beyond the realm of personal experience and is already an element of literary appreciation. The students were asked to abstract themselves from the plot and reflect on the nature of the discourse which is no mean task for seventeen- to eighteen-year-olds with little or no experience at doing so in their mother tongue. They certainly appeared to find the task taxing.

PRIOR KNOWLEDGE OF LITERARY GENRES

The last lesson on the book also contained some elements of literary appreciation although of a different nature. Students had been asked to reflect in advance on this issue: *Elise ou la vraie vie, un roman féministe?* Although the concern was not with style nor with the discourse, I nevertheless thought it was a step towards literary awareness because it meant searching the novel for the author's intentions. It also involved implicit comparisons with other feminist novels and an acquaintance with the genre. The students were unable to answer the question conclusively. What they did do, however, was list the main themes of the book and include feminism as possibly the third most important one in the novel, after racism and politics. It was obvious to me that the students did not have enough knowledge of the various literary genres and more precisely the feminist genre, to be able to give a different answer. Their response was therefore limited and the teacher did not pursue the point.

Variations, progression and evaluation

I did not encounter anywhere else a similar attempt to develop a sense of literary appreciation among the students. This does not mean that it did not take place but if it did, I did not witness it.

It is interesting to note that this incursion into literary appreciation took place in College 2 which was then following the SUJB B syllabus and for which such in-depth knowledge was not required. Teacher F told me that she only attempts such an approach with good groups, and if time allows. For her, discussing issues that stem from the books and getting students to respond to what they read takes priority.

It is also worth mentioning, even if it comes as no surprise, that the activities focusing on style, imagery and genre, took place very much at the end of the course, when the students had already read five books in class and several more independently. They had been exposed to a variety of plots and issues but also of writing styles and, consequently, they had acquired a certain reading experience allowing them to compare and relate books to one another, a little along the lines suggested by Brumfit's wider reading approach (Brumfit, 1986: 255–260).

To come back to the question of whether there was evidence that some form of literary appreciation was being encouraged among this age group in the three colleges, the answer must be no, not really.

STAYING CLEAR OF 'LIT CRIT'

Of course there were the two isolated cases which I have just referred to, but they were the exceptions rather than the rule. Teachers seemed to want to stay clear of what used to characterise the former 'lit crit' method when much was made of style, genres, literary history and the opinion of the critics. Instead they put the emphasis on personal response and enjoyment and were largely successful. Their aims were very much like Carter's when he wrote:

> 'The principal goal is to put the student inside the text so that it can be recreated in terms of personal response, an individual rather than a rehearsed account of the impact the text has on the reader.' (Carter, 1990: 220)

The students' response to the attempt at literary appreciation was not good and there was evidence that they were not coping well, possibly because they were on unfamiliar ground, and several looked bored.

It seemed therefore that the teachers of these three colleges had chosen wisely when they decided that a formal critical appreciation was not appropriate for this age group or at least not as appropriate as the opportunity to relate personally to the characters and situations in the books.

The respective roles of teachers and students in the reading lesson

Before concluding this section on classroom observation, I need to devote a little time to analyse the nature of the role played by teachers and students during the lessons I attended.

GENERAL FEATURES OF PRACTICE

The lessons I observed were all very structured and ordered. Students knew what was expected of them in class and at home and most of them seemed to do it. A few times I noticed that some had skipped homework or not done it properly and that some slipped back to English in role plays or discussions when the teacher was not near them.

The lessons were also very much student-centred. What seemed to matter was to get the class involved, to get them to reflect on what they had read, to share views, discuss with one another and with the teacher. A variety of activities was used from narrow questions to open-ended ones, role plays and whole class discussions.

I felt that the students coped adequately with the language of the texts, possibly because the choice of books had been mostly made along linguistic criteria, and progression took place along the same lines. Only in the case of *Elise ou la vraie vie* and possibly *Les petits enfants du siècle* did it become noticeable that some students were struggling and that language difficulties were 'short-circuiting' efficient processing of the text, to use Clarke's image (Clarke, 1988: 114–124). This occurred when students were confronted with unfamiliar registers: in the case of the first book there was heavy use of technical vocabulary, a register almost unknown to the students. In the second case, the heroine frequently lapsed into non-standard French rich in colloquialisms and adolescent slang. However, because she was like them an adolescent, they were able to identify with some of her problems and empathy probably alleviated some of the problems they encountered with the language. This was not the case with the character of Elise who seemed to remain much more remote to them.

GRADUAL MOVE TOWARDS AUTONOMY

Because most students appeared willing to get involved in the activities, one could almost have believed, especially towards the end of the course, that the classes run themselves and that the teacher's role was negligible. It certainly was true that the lessons were largely student-centred, but everything was carefully orchestrated by the teacher along the lines indicated by Teacher A in her interview, when she described her role as that of an *animatrice*. However, this situation was only gradually established and it required a constant effort to make students more independent and to wean them from the temptation to rely too much on their teacher.

NEGATIVE ASPECTS OF TEACHER-CENTREDNESS

I noticed one exception: in Teacher E's lesson, no group work took place and the whole session was entirely teacher-led. The students had no autonomy and were constantly either being fed information on *Les mains sales* or closely questioned to establish whether they had understood the play. The level of involvement was not high, with some students sitting back and looking a little bored while the most extrovert gave all the answers. The students also appeared to be less self-assured, asking their teacher frequently to clarify points of language or some aspect of the plot. I did wonder whether this was because they were not given the opportunity to bounce ideas off each other, or because they felt that the teacher expected them to come to him for confirmation that they were right. This reminded me very much of the traditional approach to literature when students were led to believe that there were right or wrong reactions to books. The fact that the plot and the ideas were quite complex did little to encourage independence and I did wonder to what extent this was deliberate.

However, all teachers had to be authoritarian at times in order to ensure that homework was done and that the target language was used during group work. This constant checking on the students required them to be very alert even though they mostly kept a low profile.

There were minor variations due to individual teaching styles and also group dynamics, but on the whole (with the exception of the lesson with Teacher B) the similarities were actually quite amazing. I did witness the same type of progression across the three colleges from teacher-centred and teacher-led lessons early in the course, to lessons where students were more or less expected to 'get-on with it'.

Evaluation

I felt that critics like Corless, Brumfit and Benton, who all favour a personal response to texts, would have approved of these lessons and of the way in which teachers were encouraging their students to get involved and respond individually while they themselves seemed to be there, not to transmit knowledge but to help the students interact with the texts. They seemed to work along the lines advocated by Elliott for ESL situations:

> 'At all times to try to guide the students towards their own discovery of meaning, whether personally or as a group, rather than impose the meaning on them.' (Elliott, 1990: 192)

I personally thought that the relationship teacher-student-text worked well and that the activities in use succeeded in encouraging students to interact subjectively with the texts and experience events that occured in the books.

Conclusion to the class observations

Before closing this section I would like to comment briefly on the amazing similarity between the teaching methods used by the three colleges. It puzzled me until I discovered that in each college at least three teachers had been either trained or in contact with Frank Corless who was one of the pioneers of the interactive approach to literature in the foreign language. As I mentioned earlier, his criticism, as early as 1977, of traditional examination boards and of a product-based approach to literature as totally irrelevant to the needs of sixth formers, was quite revolutionary at the time and his contribution to *French 16–19 — a new perspective* (1981) significant. Today the ideas in the booklet are widely used and many recent publications dealing with exploitation of texts in the foreign language seem to have been inspired by it. At Southampton University he was able to communicate his views to many PGCE students and two of them were among the teachers I observed.

I did not notice any major discrepancies between theory and practice, between the interviews and the class observations, and there was very little sign of the old method of teaching literature as a body of received knowledge nor of the stylistics approach based on close linguistic analysis. Once basic understanding had been established, students were encouraged to respond individually and at times imaginatively. Teachers acted mainly as mediators between the students and the text, but also between groups of students. They tried to make their experience as meaningful as possible by selecting texts which the group could tackle successfully and relate to. Their efforts were largely rewarded if the level of involvement and at times enjoyment I noticed in the lessons can be measures of success.

On the other hand, the lack of interest for an attempt at literary appreciation in College 2 by an otherwise enthusiastic group, and the difficulties experienced by the group, seem to indicate as Teacher C had pointed out in the interviews that:

'formal critical appreciation . . . is not really appropriate at the sixteen–eighteen stage.'

There is no doubt, however, that by the end of the second year all students had become competent readers of French and that the aims set by Teacher B had been reached. She had said in her interview:

'I would aim to have achieved a fairly fluent reader and for the students to have acquired strategies even if we haven't directly given them.'

CONCLUSION TO THE CASE STUDIES

The two years I spent observing students and their teachers, as well as the information given in the interviews, proved valuable to me. Not only was I able to witness a variety of teaching styles and glean ideas for my own future exploitation of literary texts, but it also very much confirmed my belief that reading literature is possible in the sixth form and can be a profitable experience for students.

The lessons that seemed to work best were the ones where:

- students were studying texts they could relate to;
- they were encouraged to interact with what they read;
- the target language was used extensively;
- there was the possibility to revert to English in certain cases.

AN INTEGRATED APPROACH

What needs to be stressed is that the study of literary texts was in all three colleges integrated with the study of the foreign language and no longer divorced, as used to happen frequently a few years ago under traditional syllabuses. The two seem to go hand in hand. Although the personal experience of students appears to be enriched and students have the opportunity to discuss issues that might not have cropped up elsewhere in the course, there is little doubt that their language proficiency is greatly improved.

The responses to a questionnaire given to students during term 5 indicate that they perceive:

- linguistic acquisition as the main benefit; followed closely by
- the ability to read at length superficially for personal reading; and
- the ability to analyse characters and plot for class reading.

Unfortunately, I did not have time to examine the results of the questionnaires for present purposes. The data I collected seemed to indicate that literary texts allow for language input as well as non-literary ones, whereas one could argue that if the main benefit seems to be linguistic, non-literary texts would do just as well. This would mean depriving our students of the possibility to respond to texts emotionally and imaginatively.

Not every one may wish, or may be able, to set aside valuable time for class-study of literary texts. There is much to cover and there is no doubt, as the teachers' interviews made clear, that our GCSE students are ill-prepared for extensive reading. However, I hope that these case studies have made it clear that it is possible for sixteen- to nineteen-year-olds to enjoy literary texts in a foreign language and to learn from them. It would be a pity therefore to deprive them of an enriching experience. I would like to encourage teachers who have reservations to give it a try, and if no class-teaching time can be found, at least to encourage personal reading of carefully selected literary texts.

References

Brumfit C J and R A Carter (eds), *Literature and language teaching* (Oxford University Press, 1986)

Brumfit C J, 'Wider reading for better reading: an alternative approach to teaching literature' in *op cit*: 256–61

Carter R A and M Long, 'Testing literature in EFL classes: tradition and innovation' in *ELT journal*, 44/3: 216–21 (Oxford University Press, 1990)

Chambers G N, 'Suggested approaches to 'A' level literature' in *Language learning journal*, 4: 5–9 (Association for Language Learning, 1991)

Clarke M A, 'The short-circuit hypothesis of ESL reading — or when language competence interferes with reading performance' in Carrell P L, J Devine and D Eskey, *Interactive approaches to second language reading* (Cambridge University Press, 1988)

Corless F, 'A new look at literary studies in the sixth form modern languages course' in *Audio-visual language journal*, 16/1: 161–9 (British Association for Language Teaching, 1978)

Elliott R, 'Encouraging reader-response to literature in ESL situations' in *English language journal*, 44/3: 191–8 (Oxford University Press, 1990)

French 16–19 Study Group, *French 16–19 — a new perspective* (Hodder and Stoughton, 1981)

Neather E J, 'The value of translations in sixth form literature teaching' in *Modern languages*, 56: 132–8 (Modern Language Association, 1975)

Conclusion

by Michael Grenfell

It is clear that Jane, Pat and Liliane are not simply teachers studying reading in their particular contexts, but are offering us information and discussion to forward the debate on reading in modern languages in the UK. In this section I add my own comments on what they carried out as teachers and the reflective methods they adopted. I also address the practice of reading in learning modern languages and consider the learner strategies that may be helpful in enhancing the effectiveness of pupils' reading habits. Finally, I make some suggestions for future topics of enquiry which readers of this book may consider as possible projects for their own reflections on practice.

Teacher researchers

Each of these reflections has been carried out by practising teachers. Each reflection demonstrates degrees of objectivity and personal involvement. Each also has their own distinct, contextual characteristics:

- Jane Roots' work is classroom-based.
- Pat Rees undertook her study within the department in which she was working.
- Liliane White went out into other colleges in order to find out what was happening elsewhere.

Both Jane and Pat undertook their reflections as a form of **action research**; as a way of developing and improving classroom practice. Liliane acted more as an objective researcher, gathering empirical evidence to find out about the attitudes to and activities surrounding reading in the sixth form.

The three contributions to this book form a series of **case studies**, which the teachers have constructed by —

- standing back from practice; and
- asking questions about what was really happening beyond their daily routines and habits.

They are practical illustrations of what can occur when teachers adopt a reflective approach to their work; in this case, to classroom practices in reading.

SIMPLE RESEARCH TECHNIQUES

In the first book to the present series (Peck and Westgate, 1994) this approach was examined and various research methods were discussed; for example, video, diaries, observation, etc. What is striking about the three teachers writing in this book is how much information was gathered by simple techniques:

- questionnaire;
- talking to pupils and students; and
- watching classroom practice carefully.

The use of:

- learner diaries

would also be appropriate to show how the various skills, problems and habits changed over time and in response to specific texts. Such detail could highlight particular learner differences and the precise outcome of various reading activities.

All of these techniques offer not only practical sources of information for teachers, who can then use them to develop their methodological approach, but also provide opportunities for the learners themselves to think about their learning in a more objective way.

REFLECTION IN L1 AS WELL AS IN L2

Reflections on language have been curiously overlooked in the fashionable trend to create monolingual classrooms; perhaps because such reflection implies a judicious use of English. Reflection of this kind is surely crucial in the process of developing learners who can take on board the strategies for learning themselves, and thus become more autonomous students.

Simple practical techniques, together with a reflective approach to the day-to-day events of classroom life can then be employed to yield fresh insights for teacher-researchers and hence more effective classroom learning.

There are distinct conclusions to be drawn from the reflections on reading offered in this book.

Reading practice

All three studies confirm the view that reading was being overlooked in lower-school language work; both in terms of quantity and quality. Pupils, it seems, were not given a varied diet of reading materials. Reading more often than not seemed to be restricted to textbooks and to short information-retrieval passages.

Moreover, pupils had not been taught how and when to read. The focus on gist understanding and getting meaning across seems to have undermined the productive, personal relationships pupils can form with language and its content. Little wonder, therefore, that, as Pat shows, the jump from GCSE to 'A' level appears so enormous. Both teachers and pupils at sixth form highlight the remedial work that has to be done in terms of language structure and the whole process of engaging with written texts. Both teachers and learners are sensitive to the need to start with simpler texts and build up. Even so, many of the texts referred to in these reflections put great demands on students as they simultaneously grapple with the book length, language sophistication and the moral dilemmas contained within. There is an evident balance to be struck between these; one that is not manifest in syllabus demands but has to be constructed between teachers and learners themselves.

Reading strategies

Implicit in the two action research studies is a classroom culture characterised not by the implementation of fixed methods of teaching or of learning but rather by notions of dialogue, negotiation and reciprocal learning. In Patricia Rees' memorable phrase, teacher and learners created together a *dialogue of discovery* that enabled each party to learn from the other. This seems close to the reflective classroom culture currently advocated by researchers such as Donato and McCormick (1994) and Lantolf (1994), writing from a sociocultural perspective in which dialogue between students and teacher plays an important mediating role in enabling learners to develop and refine their own strategies.

There are currently very many ideas for activities in reading (cf Grellet 1981, Kavanagh and Upton 1994, Swarbrick 1990). Most of these are lively and imaginative and will broaden the range and approach to reading in the classroom. Increasingly, the number of activities is not enough on its own. Rather, these need to be rethought in terms of procedure and development of language competence and corresponding reading tasks.

It is clear that lack of understanding, or misunderstanding, is an enormous barrier to pupils developing confident reading skills. A part of reading will always be literal; indeed, the literal is the window to higher evaluative, personal responses. These latter, more sophisticated, reading skills are also crucial to the development of independent readers who are capable of forming judgements in relation to texts for themselves.

This range of reading skills might be expressed in terms of Beginner; Intermediate; and Advanced levels, and the style of reading matched accordingly:

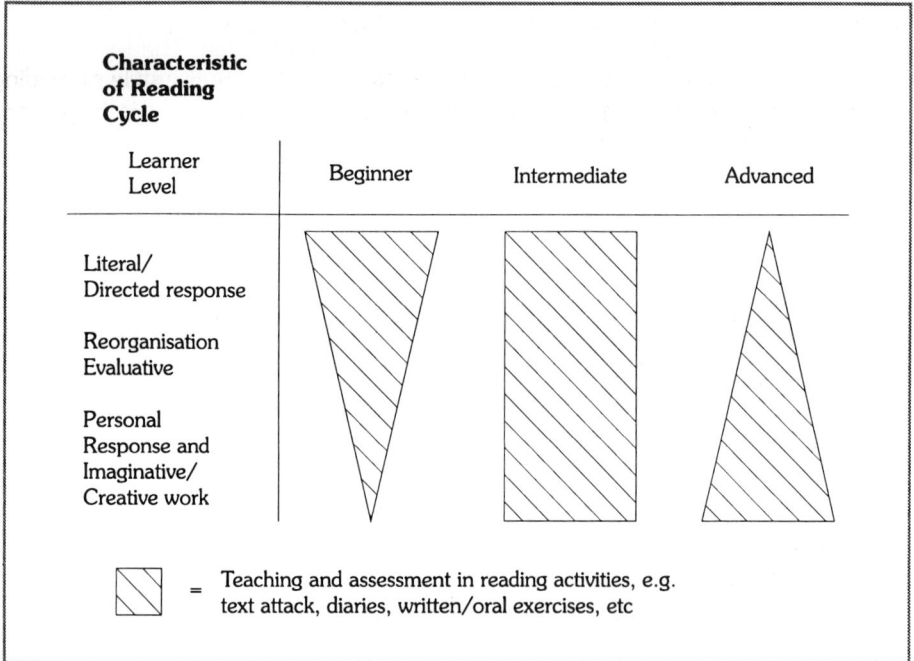

'Process reading in the communications classroom'
by Michael Grenfell: 50 (*Language Learning Journal 6*, 1992)

The important point here is that each of the characteristics of reading are represented at each of the three levels of language learning; so that at no stage is reading considered to be only literal, or only for personal response. It is rather a question of balance over the stages of learning. Necessarily, a lot of early work in reading will focus on literal, directed response and matching sounds to words. However, it is nonetheless important that opportunities for personal response are included through, for example, the emotional content of some language forms and responses to graphics, etc. Jane illustrates how this can be started with her reading access programme.

The contributions by Pat and Liliane emphasise the attempts by 'advanced' students to gain control over the texts with which they are presented; and their recourse to synopses, readers, translations, etc in order to do this. The literal should not be overlooked at this level. And yet to deal with it, students need to have developed dictionary habits and skills, and a personal balance on the degree to which to make use of these skills. Clearly, looking up every unknown word is neither feasible nor desirable. Getting a feel for knowing what and when to look things up, and the use of monolingual and bilingual dictionaries, are sophisticated skills. If students are also to respond in a personal way to the sorts of dilemmas contained within literary text, then personal response needs to be a guiding principle at an earlier stage in the language learning cycle.

Thinking of reading in these terms by examining activities for the style of reading required and by varying the purposes of reading accordingly is important developmentally. For example:

Level 1
Match oral sounds to words
Group words according to function; lexical, syntactical category, etc
Match synonyms/antonyms
Read-cover-check-write
Scan for information
Word family trees
Guess cognates
Split sentences
Words that rhyme
Answer questions or true/false statements
Skim for general ideas
Select key vocabulary, events.

Level 2
Rewrite: move from 1st to 3rd person
Label diagram or fill in table
Rearrange words/sentences/structures/paragraphs
Draw diagram from the text
Any questions: Talk to partner/class on text
Follow instructions
Modified cloze tests
Write chapter headings
Write paragraph headings
Prepare questions
Judge if language is appropriate
Judge if event is authentic: could it happen?
Evaluate certain aspects of the text/book/poem.

Level 3
Write headlines
Write script from prose or prose from script
Predict ending
Interview assumed characters
List sympathies/differences with the characters
Change ending
Picture poems
Advice to characters
Comment, positively or negatively, on atmosphere, characters, etc.

(Grenfell 1992: 51).

However, thinking of activities in these terms is only part of the solution. Besides reintegrating reading into language learning programmes, it will be necessary to think of the varied dimensions underlying certain activities:

• Firstly, the habit of reading has to be reintroduced. This will require reading programmes: reading in class and for homework. Reader diaries will be helpful here, in which activities are recorded, personal judgements made and reflections developed.
• Secondly, offering a variety of texts is the complement to learner choice in selecting what to read.
• Thirdly, teaching learners to adapt and apply reading skills to suit texts and parts thereof. For example, it is often not a question of intensive **or** extensive reading, but a combination of both within particular contexts.

Above all, reading needs to create and enhance a sense of self in relation to the text, not merely be a source of retrieved information. It is in identifying with the content of language that the biggest reinforcement to general linguistic competence will be made. For learners, reading is a shared activity; not only as a daily habit but in the creation of a community of ideas on which and through which to communicate.

Practically orientated theorising like this about reading practices can be seen here to be one of the outcomes of the reflective case writing of Jane, Pat and Liliane. Nonetheless, noticing and changing individual classroom practices remains at the core of the reflective understanding of these three teachers

Having read this book, the reader may want to undertake a similar reflection on practice themselves. In the following section I address the sort of possible projects that may be carried out by teachers in the future.

Future reflections

The reflections included in this book raise the profile of reading across a range of language learning in UK schools. Greater numbers of published readers for early learners are now coming on to the market; foreign language magazines are more accessible and available; syllabus reform at 'A' level offers greater opportunity and flexibility in approaches to text in the sixth form.

Getting hold of these materials is only the first step. Using them within a reading programme is a second step. After that, undertaking the kind of reflections on practice presented in this book will be helpful in developing effective reading practices.

These future reflections might address the following:

- what learners like and dislike about reading: what is difficult and easy;
- which reading strategies are identifiable with learners at different stages of linguistic development;
- which strategies are most effective and when;
- which strategies can be fairly easily taught — for example, dictionary skills; and which are less so — for example, automatically matching reading purpose to reading approach;
- an examination of reading activities given throughout the range of language learning in terms of developmental, procedural skills;
- an exploration of the ways in which learners personally respond to texts;
- action research based on the use of visuals in enhancing reader response;
- further work on the use of readers, translations, synopsis as a support to reading;
- contrastive work on the difference between lit crit students and those studying contemporary themes;
- work on the use of reflection (in the target language and English) as a means to developing independent learner strategies;
- the role of cultural differences in enhancing/impeding personal response.

Above all, perhaps, there is a crucial need for teachers to follow through these issues with pupils over a period of time, as it is only with this longitudinal element that we will achieve a clearer picture of individual pupils developing in their own terms. Research techniques to do this may be quite simple, as Peck and Westgate (1994) have shown us, and be based on a combination of questionnaire, interview, classroom observations, as demonstrated in this book. **Reflecting on Practice** will make teachers more critical and less likely to repeat the mistake of following past trends. Moreover, learners will eventually have more say in how and why they read. On both counts, only improved language learning can be the result.

References

Donato R and D McCormick, 'A sociocultural perspective on language learning — the role of mediation' in *The modern language journal*, no. 78/4: 453–64 (National Federation of Modern Language Teachers Association, 1994)

Grellet F, *Developing reading skills* (Cambridge University Press, 1981)

Grenfell M (1992), 'Process reading in the communicative classroom' in *Language learning journal*, no. 6: 48–52 (Association for Language Learning, 1992)

Kavanagh B and L Upton, *Creative use of texts* (CILT, 1994)

Lantolf J P, 'Sociocultural theory and second language learning' in *The modern language journal*, no. 78/4: 418–20 (National Federation of Modern Language Teachers Association, 1994)

Peck A and D Westgate (eds), *Language teaching in the mirror* (CILT, 1994)

Swarbrick A, *Reading for pleasure in a foreign language* (CILT, 1990)

The contributors

Michael Grenfell did most of his modern language teaching in London. As an active member of the Modern Language Association he organised several conferences for teachers and students; most noticeably on the 'new' non-literary 'A' level syllabuses. Since 1989 he has been Lecturer in Education in charge of Modern Languages at the Centre for Language in Education at Southampton University. He trains students, teaches on MA courses and is involved in a number of research projects. He is Co-ordinator of the Southampton Comenius Centre and is on the CILT Teacher Training Working Group. A frequent participant at conferences, he has given many talks on language teaching and learning and published widely in various journals and books.

Professor Richard Johnstone is Head of the Department of Education, University of Stirling, and Director of the Scottish Centre for Information on Language Teaching and Research (Scottish CILT). He has directed many research projects for SOIED on the teaching and learning of foreign or second languages, and has written several books on the subject. His most recent work has included responsibility for the evaluation of national pilot projects in modern languages in Scottish primary schools.

Patricia Rees is a former Head of French in a sixth form college where the research reported in this book was carried out. She is currently Visiting Fellow in the Education Faculty of Southampton University and is continuing to work in the field of learning strategies, with particular reference to reading skills. She has a general interest in educational issues and in the history of ideas. Over the years she has taught in a number of educational institutions at higher and secondary level both in England and France. At present she is lecturing part-time in adult and higher education and is an Arts tutor with the Open University.

Jane Roots is Head of Modern Languages in a comprehensive school in Hampshire. She has many years' teaching experience and has been involved in numerous local initiatives in the field. The reflective practice reported here was carried out as part of her MA studies at Southampton University. It was this course that got her thinking about the importance of reading in the modern languages classroom. In particular, she has been concerned to make use of approaches from an English context, especially poetry, and to develop a wide range of materials to encourage reading in a foreign language. She has worked extensively to find out what and how her pupils read.

Liliane White is French. She studied at Lyon University and completed her *Maîtrise de Lettres* in 1974. She works at Queen Mary's Sixth Form College in Basingstoke where she teaches on a wide range of courses. She has also taught in secondary schools and adult education. The research reported in this book formed part of an MPhil degree on the teaching and study of literary texts at French 'A' level which she completed at Southampton University in 1994.